# SPIRITUAL BOOT CAMP

# SPIRITUAL BOOT CAMP

★★★★★

KIMBERLY DANIELS

Most Charisma House Book Group products are available at special quantity discounts for bulk purchase for sales promotions, premiums, fund-raising, and educational needs. For details, write Charisma House Book Group, 600 Rinehart Road, Lake Mary, Florida 32746, or telephone (407) 333-0600.

Spiritual Boot Camp by Kimberly Daniels
Published by Charisma House
Charisma Media/Charisma House Book Group
600 Rinehart Road
Lake Mary, Florida 32746
www.charismahouse.com

Cover design by Justin Evans
Design Director: Bill Johnson

Visit the author's website at www.kimberlydaniels.com.

Library of Congress Cataloging-in-Publication Data:
An application to register this book for cataloging has been submitted to the Library of Congress.
International Standard Book Number: 978-1-61638-713-6
E-book ISBN: 978-1-61638-714-3



First edition

12 13 14 15 16 — 9 8 7 6 5 4 3 2 1
Printed in the United States of America

## Dedication

The vision of this book is to train, equip, impart, and activate believers to BE ALL THEY CAN BE...in Jesus Christ. This book is based on disciplines I learned in the military as a soldier, biblical principles, and ministerial experience I have obtained over the years. The focus of this book will be to give every believer (from the layperson to the fivefold minister) a vision to fulfill the call of God on his or her life in excellence and under authority.

In the natural new army recruits are sent to boot camp to learn how to be soldiers. Scriptures such as "The weapons of our warfare are not carnal" (2 Cor. 10:4, NKJV) and "Put on the whole armor of God" (Eph. 6:11, NKJV) clearly confirm that when we give our lives to Jesus, we enlist in God's army; we do not join a social elite club. After reading this book you will be:

---

- Trained and equipped to be soldiers in the army of the Lord
- Ignited or reignited with the fire of God to assure that you will never become weary in well-doing
- Empowered to reach out to the lost
- Activated to share what you have learned with a fellow brother or sister in the Lord

---

Because we are soldiers, it is important to understand that as soldiers we have a duty assignment. Whenever one vision (the vision of the kingdom) has to be completed with many people assigned to the task, there has to be order. In the natural the military is founded on order. In comparison the kingdom of God is also rooted in order.

*Spiritual Boot Camp* will give information to release a better understanding of *apostolic ministry* and the importance of *prophetic ministry* in the days we live in. Since these are the foundational ministries in the household of faith, this book will touch on all the gifts that God has given to the church for the perfecting of the saints. For our churches to be prepared for the end-time challenges ahead, individual believers must be trained, equipped, and ready to walk in spiritual maturity.

We have experienced the dangers of the idolatrous superstar personalities in the church. This book will highlight the importance of the anointing on the congregation of the Lord. This book puts pressure on fivefold ministry gifts (term used to identify spiritual leaders) to get in place and prepare for the overall vision of the kingdom. To do this, we must get back to the basics of the simplicity of the gospel of Jesus Christ so that the church will be ready for the next level of glory.

This book is dedicated to soldiers whom I had close interaction with who received *early releases* from duty. They ended their tours of duty earlier than we thought should have happened, but God knew the days of their tour before they were formed in their mothers' wombs:

- Ardell Daniels II
- Whitney Houston
- James Bailey
- Aaron Terry
- Brother Jeff

You have finished your course and have joined the ranks of the cloud of witnesses in the third heaven. We miss you!

# Contents

# Foreword

THE ANCIENT WARRIOR culture of Sparta was one in which every male was trained in the tactics and individual skills of the soldier. Young boys were taken from their families at an early age (six years old) and trained as warriors through an extremely difficult regimen that included physical fitness and strength training as well as basic survival and wrestling. The training was progressive, reaching its crescendo with team work and combat skills by the time they were thirteen years old. This training and the discipline and selfless commitment that was inculcated into these fierce soldiers made them legendary in the annals of military history. As they stood with their great King Leonidas, facing the army of the Persian King Xerxes in 480 B.C., the outcome of the impending battle was predictable. The 300 Spartans were destined to lose the battle because they were confronting an army of over 250,000 Persian warriors. Staged for battle at a place called Thermopylae, there was no chance of a Spartan victory in this small mountain pass along the coast of Greece. But the battle that ensued became one of the most famous in history as the 300 men in the Spartan army held off the mighty army of Xerxes for three days, inflicting heavy casualties on the Persians and giving the Greek city-states time to evacuate their towns and to regroup for a future naval battle. Although King Leonidas and his men all died in the battle of Thermopylae, they inflicted a heavy toll on the Persians and set the stage for a subsequent victory by the Greeks later in 480 B.C. at the Battle of Salamis, where the Persians were defeated. The story becomes even more intriguing because King Leonidas was offered the opportunity to surrender rather than die in a futile effort. With a promise of leniency by King Xerxes, King Leonidas was asked to lay down his weapons by an emissary of the Persian king. King Leonidas responded with a simple retort: "*Molon lebe,*" or "Come and take them."

Exodus 15:3 says, "The Lord is a Man of War," and Revelation 19 describes Jesus as a warrior riding a white horse with a blood-stained white robe as He commands a great army fighting against His enemies to ultimately annihilate them. It therefore seems reasonable that we as Christians are expected to be an army for the Lord. We are God's warriors, and we need to be trained as the ancient Spartans were. We need to be placed in a spiritual "boot camp" in order to be in God's army. But where do we find this kind of training?

Today there are many people who consider themselves Christians but who are totally unprepared to serve God and to find and do His will in their lives. Furthermore, they are ill-prepared to engage in the spiritual warfare that each Christian encounters in doing God's work. Therefore much of the church is lethargic and not engaged in the struggle for souls. Many Christians are struggling in their faith walk and have yet to know what God expects of them or how God wants to use them. Although they have a desire to go into battle for the kingdom, they are just simply not prepared.

Apostle Kimberly Daniels is a warrior of the "Spartan" class. Not only has she served in the United States Army, but she is also a spiritual warrior of the highest order who is in the fight every day, slaying dragons and, like Leonidas, challenging the enemy. "*Molon lebe,*" she shouts at evil. She is fearless in her fight for justice and for the kingdom of God. Now she shares her wisdom and experience in this book in an effort to help Christians to prepare for service to the King. Reflecting on her own military boot-camp experiences and her incredible journey from cocaine addiction to elected office, Kimberly lays out the fundamentals of how to prepare for service to the Lord. The Christian church needs modern Spartans, and this former street-wise-addict-turned-minister-of-the-gospel lays out how to adorn ourselves with the whole armor of God. Step by step she takes the reader through the process of becoming a strong warrior for the kingdom—a Spartan.

—Lieutenant General (Ret) William G. "Jerry" Boykin

*LTG (Ret) Jerry Boykin was one of the original members of the US Army's Delta Force. He was privileged to ultimately command these elite warriors in combat operations. Later, Jerry Boykin commanded all the Army's Green Berets. He has participated in clandestine operations around the world. Today he is an ordained minister with a passion for spreading the gospel of Jesus Christ.*

## Introduction

# BOOT CAMP INDUCTION

Because of the day we live in, spiritual discipline is a priority. Economic issues, cultural concerns, the struggle for power, and the war of religion steer the ship on the course of this world. As believers, in order to understand what is working for us, we must get a revelation of what is working against us. When I went to basic training in Fort Jackson, South Carolina, I was introduced to the military by being put on a cattle truck (like an animal) with a few shell-shocked drill sergeants. Their assignment was to introduce the new trainees to the reality of the fact that they were no longer in the civilian world. The drill sergeants screamed and got in the faces of the trainees to break them as they ran around trying to find their personal duffle bags in the midst of seventy other enlistees. It was a rude awakening! We were no longer civilians; we belonged to Uncle Sam. Being an adult did not matter; we had to become as children and follow the orders of the drills. *Drill sergeants* are so named because they are charged to drill (or instill) principles in the minds of trainees to transform them into soldiers.

As the drill sergeants yelled at me, I was not moved. With my street mentality I looked at them like a bunch of geeks with stupid hats on their heads. Those hats represented more than my limited mind-set could imagine. Because I did not respect the *hat(s)*, I went through more than I had to during my eight weeks of training.

A spot in Drill Sergeant School is one of the highest honors the US Army can bestow upon a noncommissioned officer (NCO). Only the most qualified NCOs are chosen to attend Drill Sergeant School, where they are trained to fulfill a role of utmost importance—the role of a drill sergeant. After all, drill sergeants teach new recruits every aspect of basic combat training (BCT)—which means they have the great responsibility of shaping recruits into the best soldiers in the world.

NCOs who attend Drill Sergeant School are called drill sergeant candidates. Their training is strenuous. The school's curriculum mimics basic combat training, week for week, because candidates must become experts in all facets of BCT to begin training recruits. They receive top-notch training from their drill sergeant instructors because they will soon be expected to deliver great training.

For many candidates, becoming a drill sergeant is a *military dream*. It means they have proven themselves again and again—so much so that they're entrusted with training new recruits. They know that when they receive their drill sergeant hat, they'll have the ultimate job—being a role model—and they take it very seriously.

Earning the drill sergeant's hat is not easy. When NCOs are tapped to attend Drill Sergeant School, they know they'll have to be able to teach new recruits the proper way to do absolutely everything in the army—from making a bed, to wearing a uniform, to firing a rifle. They will have to become the best, because US Army recruits deserve to learn from the best. In the end drill sergeants are instantly recognizable. The hat of the drill sergeant represents honor and authority. Trainees encounter many noncommissioned officers, but when the man with the drill hat approaches, it requires another level of attention.

Spiritually speaking I cannot write this book on boot camp as just a preacher or minister. God allowed me to be a noncommissioned officer (NCO) in the United States Army so that I could draw from the training and authority that was imparted to me in my seven years of service. Just as the drill sergeant received the hat, God gives mantles. There must be an apostolic authority and a designated mantle from the Lord to train people who will someday train others in the way of the Lord.

In the name of Jesus I put on my spiritual drill hat and pray that you will get under the covering of what God is releasing through this book and walk in the generational authority of it. God says that we must come to Him as children when it comes to the things of His Word. No matter how long you have been saved or what your title is, I pray that you will enter into the boot camp of the Lord as a private. When we humble ourselves under the mighty hand of the Lord, spiritual promotion comes in due season.

Just as a new inductee in the United States Army stands before an army official and is charged with the reasons for and qualifications of becoming a soldier in the army, our *Field Manual*—the Holy Bible—charges spiritual inductees with the reasons for becoming a member of God's army and gives the qualifications and standards by which God's soldiers must abide. The following portions of Scripture from our *Field Manual* are your charge into God's army as we begin this book.

---

**INDUCTEE'S CHARGE INTO GOD'S ARMY**

> But understand this, that in the last days will come (set in) perilous times of great stress and trouble [hard to deal with and hard to bear]. For people will be lovers of self and [utterly] self-centered, lovers of money and aroused by an inordinate [greedy] desire for wealth, proud and arrogant and contemptuous boasters. They will be abusive (blasphemous, scoffing), disobedient to parents, ungrateful, unholy and profane. [They will be] without natural [human] affection (callous and inhuman), relentless (admitting of no truce or appeasement); [they will be] slanderers (false accusers, troublemakers), intemperate and loose in morals and conduct, uncontrolled and fierce, haters of good. [They will be] treacherous [betrayers], rash, [and] inflated with self-conceit. [They will be] lovers of sensual pleasures and vain amusements more than and rather than lovers of God.
>
> For [although] they hold a form of piety (true religion), they deny and reject and are strangers to the power of it [their conduct belies the genuineness of their profession]. Avoid [all] such people [turn away from them].
>
> ...All who delight in piety and are determined to live a devoted and godly

life in Christ Jesus will meet with persecution [will be made to suffer because of their religious stand]. But wicked men and imposters will go on from bad to worse, deceiving and leading astray others and being deceived and led astray themselves. But as for you, continue to hold to the things that you have learned and of which you are convinced, knowing from whom you learned [them], and how from your childhood you have had a knowledge of and been acquainted with the sacred Writings, which are able to instruct you and give you the understanding for salvation which comes through faith in Christ Jesus [through the leaning of the entire human personality on God in Christ Jesus in absolute trust and confidence in His power, wisdom, and goodness].

Every Scripture is God-breathed (given by His inspiration) and profitable for instruction, for reproof and conviction of sin, for correction of error and discipline in obedience, [and] for training in righteousness (in holy living, in conformity to God's will in thought, purpose, and action), so that the man of God may be complete and proficient well fitted and thoroughly equipped for every good work.

—2 TIMOTHY 3:1–5, 12–17

I charge [you] in the presence of God and of Christ Jesus, Who is to judge the living and the dead, and by (in the light of) His coming and His kingdom: Herald and preach the Word! Keep your sense of urgency [stand by, be at hand and ready], whether the opportunity seems to be favorable or unfavorable. [Whether it is convenient or inconvenient, whether it is welcome or unwelcome, you as preacher of the Word are to show people in what way their lives are wrong.] And convince them, rebuking and correcting, warning and urging and encouraging them, being unflagging and inexhaustible in patience and teaching. For the time is coming when [people] will not tolerate (endure) sound and wholesome instruction, but, having ears itching [for something pleasing and gratifying], they will gather to themselves one teacher after another to a considerable number, chosen to satisfy their own liking and to foster the errors they hold, and will turn aside from hearing the truth and wander off into myths and man-made fictions.

As for you be calm and cool and steady, accept and suffer unflinchingly every hardship, do the work of an evangelist, fully perform all the duties of your ministry. For I am already about to be sacrificed [my life is about to be poured out as a drink offering]; the time of my [spirit's] release [from the

> body] is at hand and I will soon go free. I have fought the good (worthy, honorable, and noble) fight, I have finished the race, I have kept (firmly held) the faith. [As to what remains] henceforth there is laid up for me the [victor's] crown of righteousness [for being right with God and doing right], which the Lord, the righteous Judge, will award to me and recompense me on that [great] day—and not to me only, but also to all those who have loved and yearned for and welcomed His appearing (His return).
>
> —2 TIMOTHY 4:1–8

---

## Oath of Enlistment Into God's Army

(Raise both hands to the Lord)

I, (repeat your name), renounce my flesh, the world, and every demonic realm that would hinder me from being all that I can be in Christ Jesus. I vow to serve the Lord Jesus Christ with all my heart and soul and to be a gatekeeper in the kingdom and a contender of the faith. I will carry out every mission with excellence and submit my members to God first and then to those He has put in my life to rule over me. I renounce all past habits that would entangle me with people, places, and things to distract me from the vision of my calling. I submit myself to prayer, the studying of our operations guidebook—the Word of God—and to praise and worship as a lifestyle. I commit to love not my life unto death as I seek first the kingdom of God and His righteousness. I will purpose to love and serve God's people with the agape love of God. My heart is prepared to walk in faith and receive the benefits of my enlistment. I believe that as I serve the Lord, He will provide for all of my needs according to His riches in glory. I give my family, possessions, and cares to the Lord, for He cares for me. Just as He oversees the lilies of the field, He will oversee my affairs.

I put on my spiritual gear—the helmet of salvation, the breastplate of righteousness, and the belt of truth. My feet are shod with the preparation of the gospel of peace; in one hand I carry the sword of the Spirit and in the other the shield of faith. The blood of Jesus covers all that concerns me and everything I am assigned to do. I declare that when I am weak, God will be my strength, and when I am poor in any area of my life, He will be my wealth. Goodness and mercy shall follow me all the days of my life, and I will dwell in the house (army) of the Lord forever. Amen.

______________________________

SIGNATURE

______________________________

DATE

# PART ONE

# THE IMPORTANCE OF GOD'S ARMY

All members of God's army must have a basis of understanding for what God's kingdom is and what defines the characteristics of God's soldiers. It is vital to recognize that the source of all spiritual strength and power comes through faith and trust in our Father God, our Savior and Lord Christ Jesus, and His Holy Spirit's direction and revelation. Biblical values influence God's soldier's character and spiritual development, instilling a desire to acquire the essential spiritual knowledge to fulfill God's purposes on earth. This section introduces the Christian soldier to the fundamentals of God's army and the importance of being ready to do spiritual battle in our world today.

## Chapter 1

# THE BASILICA OF GOD

THE GOVERNMENT OF God cannot be understood without addressing the kingdom of God. The Greek word for "kingdom" is *basilica*. The basilica of God is threefold in nature:

---

1. *Internal*—that which abides inside the heart of men
2. *External*—that which manifests in the earth realm through God inside of men
3. *Eternal*—that which pertains to everlasting life in Jesus Christ, which is awarded to those who endure to the end

---

Based on these three aspects of the kingdom, it is safe to define the kingdom as: "A resident anointing that lives in the hearts of men after they are spiritually born again." Because the greater One lives on the inside, they are in the world but not of it. This new birth experience ignites the power and authority of God (in men) in the earth realm that manifests His kingdom and His will. Those who finish the course of their new life experience in this present age inherit an eternal kingdom that is everlasting. All of creation hungers for the manifestation of the kingdom of God coming to earth, as it is in heaven. This manifestation will only come through the true sons and daughters of God. The manifestation of the true sons and daughters of God will expose the counterfeits. This is one of the greatest needs we have as believers in the end time. Real counterfeits are carbon copies of the genuine thing. If it is possible, even the elect will be deceived.

This revelation separates the kingdom from the church. We have problems in the church, but the basilica of God is not subject to those problems. This is when the church will be prepared for the return of the Lord Jesus. *He is coming back for a church without spot, wrinkle, or blemish.* This cleansing and ironing out of the house of God will come with a revelation of the basilica of God.

It is absolutely vital that God's soldier know what our spiritual operations guidebook—God's Word—reveals about the basilica—kingdom—of God. As a first step in your training for service in God's army, take the time now to review some of the important information in our operations guidebook about God's kingdom.

---

## SCRIPTURES ON THE KINGDOM

> Blessed (happy, to be envied, and spiritually prosperous—with life-joy and satisfaction in God's favor and salvation, regardless of their outward conditions) are the poor in spirit (the humble, who rate themselves insignificant), for theirs is the kingdom of heaven!
>
> —MATTHEW 5:3

> Blessed and happy and enviably fortunate and spiritually prosperous (in the state in which the born-again child of God enjoys and finds satisfaction in God's favor and salvation, regardless of his outward conditions) are those who are persecuted for righteousness' sake (for being and doing right), for theirs is the kingdom of heaven!
>
> —MATTHEW 5:10

Whoever then breaks or does away with or relaxes one of the least [important] of these commandments and teaches men so shall be called least [important] in the kingdom of heaven, but he who practices them and teaches others to do so shall be called great in the kingdom of heaven.

—MATTHEW 5:19

For I tell you, unless your righteousness (your uprightness and your right standing with God) is more than that of the scribes and Pharisees, you will never enter the kingdom of heaven.

—MATTHEW 5:20

Your kingdom come, Your will be done on earth as it is in heaven.

—MATTHEW 6:10

And lead (bring) us not into temptation, but deliver us from the evil one. For Yours is the kingdom and the power and the glory forever. Amen.

—MATTHEW 6:13

But seek (aim at and strive after) first of all His kingdom and His righteousness (His way of doing and being right), and then all these things taken together will be given you besides.

—MATTHEW 6:33

And Jesus went about all the cities and villages, teaching in their synagogues and proclaiming the good news (the Gospel) of the kingdom and curing all kinds of disease and every weakness and infirmity.

—MATTHEW 9:35

And as you go, preach, saying, The kingdom of heaven is at hand!

—MATTHEW 10:7

And into whatever town or village you go, inquire who in it is deserving, and stay there [at his house] until you leave [that vicinity]. As you go into the house, give your greetings and wish it well.

—MATTHEW 10:11–12

And knowing their thoughts, He said to them, Any kingdom that is divided against itself is being brought to desolation and laid waste, and no city or house divided against itself will last or continue to stand. And if Satan drives out Satan, he has become divided against himself and disunified; how then will his kingdom last or continue to stand? And if I drive out the demons by [help of] Beelzebub, by whose [help] do your sons drive them out? For this reason they shall be your judges. But if it is by the Spirit of God that I drive out the demons, then the kingdom of God has come upon you [before you expected it].

—MATTHEW 12:25–28

And He replied to them, To you it has been given to know the secrets and mysteries of the kingdom of heaven, but to them it has not been given.

—MATTHEW 13:11

While anyone is hearing the Word of the kingdom and does not grasp and comprehend it, the evil one comes and snatches away what was sown in his heart. This is what was sown along the roadside. As for what was sown on thin (rocky) soil, this is he who hears the Word and at once welcomes and accepts it with joy; yet it has no real root in him, but is temporary (inconstant, lasts but a little while); and when affliction or trouble or persecution comes on account of the Word, at once he is caused to stumble [he is repelled and begins to distrust and desert Him Whom he ought to trust and obey] and he falls away.

As for what was sown among thorns, this is he who hears the Word, but the cares of the world and the pleasure and delight and glamour and deceitfulness of riches choke and suffocate the Word, and it yields no fruit. As for what was sown on good soil, this is he who hears the Word and grasps and comprehends it; he indeed bears fruit and yields in one case a hundred times as much as was sown, in another sixty times as much, and in another thirty.

—MATTHEW 13:19–23

Another parable He set forth before them, saying, The kingdom of heaven is like a man who sowed good seed in his field. But while he was sleeping, his enemy came and sowed also darnel (weeds resembling wheat) among the wheat, and went on his way. So when the plants sprouted and formed grain, the darnel (weeds) appeared also. And the servants of the owner came to him and said, Sir, did you not sow good seed in your field? Then how does it have darnel shoots in it? He replied to them, An enemy has done this. The servants said to him, Then do you want us to go and weed them out? But he said, No, lest in gathering the wild wheat (weeds resembling wheat), you root up the [true] wheat along with it. Let them grow together until the harvest; and at harvest time I will say to the reapers, Gather the darnel first and bind it in bundles to be burned, but gather the wheat into my granary.

—MATTHEW 13:24–30

Another story by way of comparison He set forth before them, saying, The kingdom of heaven is like a grain of mustard seed, which a man took and sowed in his field. Of all the seeds it is the smallest, but when it has grown it is the largest of the garden herbs and becomes a tree, so that the birds of the air come and find shelter in its branches. He told them another parable: The kingdom of heaven is like leaven (sour dough) which a woman took and covered over in three measures of meal or flour till all of it was leavened.

These things all taken together Jesus said to the crowds in parables; indeed, without a parable He said nothing to them. This was in fulfillment of what was spoken by the prophet: I will open My mouth in parables; I will utter things that have been hidden since the foundation of the world. Then He left the throngs and went into the house. And His disciples came to Him saying, Explain to us the parable of the darnel in the field.

He answered, He Who sows the good seed is the Son of Man. The field is the world, and the good seed means the children of the kingdom; the darnel is the children of the evil one.

—MATTHEW 13:31–38

The kingdom of heaven is like something precious buried in a field, which a man found and hid again; then in his joy he goes and sells all he has and buys that field. Again the kingdom of heaven is like a man who is a dealer in search of fine and precious pearls, who, on finding a single pearl of great price, went and sold all he had and bought it. Again, the kingdom of heaven is like a dragnet which was cast into the sea and gathered in fish of every sort. When it was full, men dragged it up on the beach, and sat down and sorted out the good fish into baskets, but the worthless ones they threw away. So it will be at the close and consummation of the age. The angels will go forth and separate the wicked from the righteous (those who are upright and in right standing with God) and cast them [the wicked] into the furnace of fire; there will be weeping and wailing and grinding of teeth.

Have you understood all these things [parables] taken together? They said to Him, Yes, Lord. He said to them, Therefore every teacher and interpreter of the Sacred Writings who has been instructed about and trained for the kingdom of heaven and has become a disciple is like a householder who brings forth out of his storehouse treasure that is new and [treasure that is] old [the fresh as well as the familiar].

—MATTHEW 13:44–52

For the kingdom of heaven is like the owner of an estate who went out in the morning along with the dawn to hire workmen for his vineyard.

—MATTHEW 20:1

And this good news of the kingdom (the Gospel) will be preached throughout the whole world as a testimony to all the nations, and then will come the end.

—MATTHEW 24:14

To them also He showed Himself alive after His passion (His suffering in the garden and on the cross) by [a series of] many convincing demonstrations [unquestionable evidences and infallible proofs], appearing to them during forty days and talking [to them] about the things of the kingdom of God.

—ACTS 1:3

Preaching to them the kingdom of God and teaching them about the Lord Jesus Christ with boldness and quite openly, and without being molested or hindered.

—ACTS 28:31

[After all] the kingdom of God is not a matter of [getting the] food and drink [one likes], but instead it is righteousness (that state which makes a person acceptable to God) and [heart] peace and joy in the Holy Spirit.

—ROMANS 14:17

For the kingdom of God consists of and is based on not talk but power (moral power and excellence of soul).

—1 CORINTHIANS 4:20

But I tell you this, brethren, flesh and blood cannot [become partakers of eternal salvation and] inherit or share in the kingdom of God; nor does the perishable (that which is decaying) inherit or share in the imperishable (the immortal).

—1 CORINTHIANS 15:50

But as to the Son, He says to Him, Your throne, O God, is forever and ever (to the ages of the ages), and the scepter of Your kingdom is a scepter of absolute righteousness (of justice and straightforwardness).

—HEBREWS 1:8

Let us therefore, receiving a kingdom that is firm and stable and cannot be shaken, offer to God pleasing service and acceptable worship, with modesty and pious care and godly fear and awe.

—HEBREWS 12:28

Listen, my beloved brethren: Has not God chosen those who are poor in the eyes of the world to be rich in faith and in their position as believers and to inherit the kingdom which He has promised to those who love Him?

—JAMES 2:5

Thus there will be richly and abundantly provided for you entry into the eternal kingdom of our Lord and Savior Jesus Christ.

—2 PETER 1:11

I, John, your brother and companion (sharer and participator) with you in the tribulation and kingdom and patient endurance [which are] in Jesus Christ, was on the isle called Patmos, [banished] on account of [my witnessing to] the Word of God and the testimony (the proof, the evidence) for Jesus Christ.

—REVELATION 1:9

## Chapter 2

# SPIRITUAL READINESS

My years of experience in the United States Amy and my competition as a former world-class sprinter gave me principles and strategies that have helped me to operate in my personal ministry, train and activate ministerial teams, and complete so many assignments given to me by the Lord. As a former world-class sprinter I have a great understanding of the discipline required of an athlete to maintain a level of competition readiness. Jumping high or running fast did not seal my championship; it was necessary to maintain a level of competitive readiness, which included being:

---

- Physically ready
- Mentally ready
- Provisionally ready

---

My mind and body had to be trained for the competition. I had to see the victory before I arrived at the track meet. I would run my race in my mind so many times before I actually got into my starting block.

The warm-up process was the most important part of the race. Competing with cold, stiff muscles was a sure way to end my career through injury. My warm-up process for practice was the same as my warm-up for competition. Every practice was a competition in my mind. If I was not competing against my warm-up partner, I was competing against myself. My goal was always to do better than I did the last time. Every new practice was a competition against the times I ran in my last practice. Sometimes just completing a difficult workout was the victory I needed for the day.

My warm-up consisted of jogging one mile and doing stretching exercises, drills, and wind sprints. This took a minimum of one hour to finish. For most people this would be the entire workout for the day. For a champion sprinter, this was required before the workout. My body had to be covered in a sweat suit whether it was summer or winter. The goal was to break a sweat and loosen my muscles to be able to endure the regiment of the workout for the day.

It is easy for me to compare this discipline to what we do in ministry. Many people come to church cold and stiff in the spirit. They have not warmed up in their own prayer life before coming to church to receive ministry and, in many cases, even before ministering to others. As believers we should be prepared to give or receive the word of the Lord in ministry. We must be spiritually covered so that we will not pull a muscle in the spirit and end up unfit to finish the race.

Comparing the warm-up process to preparation for battle, soldiers must be physically and mentally prepared for war. The Department of the Army assures that soldiers are provisionally taken care of by making sure they have salaries and benefits that give them peace of mind while they are in battle. It would be a horrible thing for a soldier to have to worry about his family being evicted from their home or having no food to eat while he or she is risking his or her life in battle for the country. A needy soldier is a distracted soldier. Financial stability is the will of the Lord for His troops. He says that He will supply all of their needs according to His riches in glory. Many intercessors, ministers, and members of the body of Christ get detoured from the vision that God has given them through financial attacks. I am not saying that there will not be financial challenges. I am saying that ongoing financial challenges are the greatest way soldiers are pulled from the front lines of the Lord.

Paying tithes and giving offerings are basic training disciplines that must be instilled. How can a soldier who robs the Lord fight in battle for the Lord?

## Preparation for War

This field manual will establish the preparations necessary to be a part of God's army. A part of your preparation for becoming a soldier ready for spiritual war includes:

---

1. *Having a clean weapon.* You are a weapon in the hand of the Lord. It is important that your hands and heart are clean and clear before the Lord.
2. *Having extra ammunition.* It is important that you diligently study your operations manual, the Word of the Lord. You cannot use the Word from yesterday for today. The mercy of the Lord is new every morning. You should seek the face of the Lord for fresh spiritual ammunition. Though words from the past will be in your spiritual arsenal, you must stay tuned in for present-day truth on a daily basis. Just as your physical body needs daily nutrition, you need the daily nutrition of the Word of the Lord. This same nutrition is stored in your spirit as ammunition for the battles in life.
3. *Wearing the proper uniform.* The way that God's soldier dresses for battle is by putting on the whole armor of God and by applying the blood of Jesus to your life and circumstances.
4. *The maintenance of gear.* Many believers get delivered from the sinful world and do not realize that they need to maintain their deliverance. You must walk out your salvation with fear and trembling. The

fear of God is the foundation for spiritual maintenance. Because we all fall short of God's glory, it is important to follow the instructions of Romans 12 by:

*Presenting* your body a living sacrifice, holy and acceptable to God, which is your reasonable service (v. 1).

*Not* becoming conformed to the world, but being transformed by the continual renewing of your mind (v. 2).

*Proving* what is the good, acceptable, and perfect will of God, so you will know the will of God for yourself (v. 2)

*Not* having an exaggerated opinion of your own importance (recognizing you are one soldier in a mighty, vast army) or abilities (vv. 3–4).

Remembering that God has given to you a specific measure of faith to use the specific gifts (faculties, talents, qualities) He birthed in you (vv. 3, 6).

---

Whether you serve in God's army as a lay member or a minister, you must remember that you are a servant of the Lord, called to serve His people. The military defines *service* with terms such as *military service*, *tour of duty*, *servicemen*, and *servicewomen.*

In God's army your service is unto the Lord, and you must complete the duties assigned to you by your calling and God's vision. You are called to serve the Most High God—the Commander of the army—in excellence and with joy. The commandments of the Lord are not grievous to His troops because the mission is bigger than they are.

## Spiritual Activation

Faith without works is dead. Many believers spend most of their spiritual or ministerial lives preparing for what they never really do. The Bible says that signs should follow believers. It also says that after the Word is preached, it should be confirmed with signs following. Many run after signs, but my question to you is: "Are signs *following* you?" After you have trained, studied, fasted, prayed, and attended seminars and colleges... ARE YOU DOING WHAT YOU LEARNED TO DO?

We cannot make signs follow us. When we get in place in obedience to the Lord, He equips us, and signs confirm that He is with us. Even signs that manifest must be tried by the Spirit of God, because we are in the last days. There will be lying signs and false wonders. Do not be overly concerned. When we walk in and with the real thing, we will be able to discern the false automatically. The key is not to get ahead of God; we must have patience to wait on Him and not be anxious for anything. Anxiousness is a demonic assignment against our discernment.

The Holy Spirit has set the fivefold ministry gifts in place to equip and train the body of Christ. Impartation and activation are the ultimate goal. The prophet Elisha took his gift to the grave, and even there it was effective to raise a dead man (2 Kings 13:21). God anoints us to release and reproduce of our own kind. It is very selfish for us to walk in the blessings and the power of God and not take joy in releasing it to those who walk with us. The ministers in my church in Jacksonville, Florida, are reaping the benefit of leaders who are not afraid to equip and impart to them. People travel from around the world to come to the church in Jacksonville, and they are never disappointed when I am not there. This is what apostolic ministry is all about.

Strategically speaking, spiritual activation is also released to people and teams for specific assignments. For conferences or team travel, we take time for preparation by fasting, prayer, strategic planning, administrative preparation, and networking with other ministries, teams, or cities. By the time ministry is put into action, only those involved behind the scenes (the rear detachment) and on the front lines know the work that has been put in.

## Spiritual Deactivation

To spiritually deactivate (the military term) or to cool down (the athletic term) is simply the way you transition from the ministry assignment. Like an athlete who has been in a competition, a cool-down is just as important as a warm-up. After every race it was a discipline for me to put my sweat suit on and jog two to three laps around the track to cool down. After a military assignment in the field we had a time of deactivation. This included things such as cleaning weapons, unpacking and storing equipment, and doing maintenance on vehicles.

Our ministry teams cool down or deactivate by prayer. We usually bind all backlash, retaliation, and revenge of the enemy at this time. Our conferences usually end with prophetic worship in the sanctuary while others are tearing down, packing, cleaning, and clearing out our ministry areas.

All of the disciplines that I have mentioned provide maintenance and prevent injuries in the natural sense. Applying them to our spiritual disciplines works just as well.

One of the most important aspects of deactivation is being able to make the transition from being the pastor, apostle, or prophet to being the father or mother, husband or wife, or friend. This is one of the most difficult things for people to do when God anoints them to walk in His supernatural power to bless His people. Deactivation or transition is a must. Though we never lay our gifts down, we must be able to relate to our loved ones in a way that will not make them resent being in a family of ministry.

I have counseled many families that have judges, lawyers, policemen, or other positions of authority who are not able to take off the robes or uniforms to transition into the family member that their loved ones need. When my husband needs attention, he does not need the councilwoman or apostle to attend to him. My children need to be able to relate to me as their mother more than me being their pastor. I have friends who do not need to deal with the international speaker all the time. Sometimes they just need a friend. These are the fruits of spiritual deactivation.

As you continue reading this field manual, you will find instruction and training in three important levels of spiritual readiness.

---

**LEVELS OF COMBAT READINESS**

- *Level 1*—To cause to be combat ready, assuring that all spiritual and physical requirements are met to support the battle vision
- *Level 2*—To set the vision in motion according to all that has been planned (always being open to the leading of the Holy Spirit's *military changes*)
- *Level 3*—A sealing of the mission, offsetting backlash and retaliation, and making a conscious effort toward decontamination and closing of all doors that would allow reinforcement enemy attack

---

## Important Terms

Any military operation without effective *recon* and *decon* will ultimately end in disaster. These terms are military prefixes for:

---

1. *Reconnaissance*—an exploration or inspection of an area formulated to gather military information
2. *Decontamination*—to make safe by eliminating anything harmful that may attach or contaminate

---

As you read through the pages of this field manual, I pray that you will: *Be All That You Can Be in the Holy Ghost!* You can do all things through Jesus Christ, who strengthens you. You are a mighty man or woman of valor.

There is no male or female in the Spirit. When it comes to the spirit of valor, men are called *mighty men of valor* and women are called *virtuous women*. The words *virtuous* and *valor* are the same Hebrew word: *chayil*. God called people of all races, genders, and backgrounds to do His work. "God shows no partiality and is no respecter of persons" (Acts 10:34).

## Expanded Training Materials for Study

Valor is the main ingredient in the life of the believer to create a warfare mentality to deal with the attacks that come along with the assignment of being a soldier in the army of the Lord. The Hebrew word *chayil* means to be war worthy. It also means to be strengthened with ability, wealth, resources, and might. This word is designated for a band of soldiers who are valiant and considered a strong force to be reckoned with.

No matter what your status is, you must know who you are as a soldier in the army of the Lord. The study materials in Appendix A, "Section 2-1: Spiritual Readiness" relate to the importance of valor to the soldier in God's army. Before you progress to chapter 3 of this field manual, your assignment is to read these passages until they permeate your spirit man. Pray a prayer of decree and declaration that lines up with the content of these scriptures. Allow God to soak you in the vision of being a mighty man or woman of valor. This spiritual exercise will give you a new boldness to obey God.

# PART TWO

## CHARACTERISTICS OF GOD'S SOLDIER

Just as the soldier in the United States Army is to exhibit the characteristics that identify him or her as a soldier, the believer must also be able to be identified by the characteristics that our Commander, God, wants His soldiers to exemplify. This section will discuss those characteristics and will give you the time to study and reflect upon your own life and character to see if you reflect His distinguishing characteristics. By the time you complete this section, you will be prepared to live with these instilled characteristics, demonstrating them in all your actions and activities. You cannot be His soldier without His characteristics expressed in everything you do.

## Chapter 3

# THE IMPORTANCE OF A GOOD FOUNDATION

WHEN YOUNG MEN and women volunteer for enlistment in the United States Army, those individuals commit themselves to the rigorous training needed to prepare to *be all that they can be* according to the standards of the military. It will require the intensive demands of basic combat training—*boot camp*—where they not only learn what the army is all about and how to use weapons, but they also learn to understand and uphold the core values that make them soldiers.

There are seven core army values they are taught. These include:

---

- *Loyalty*—bearing true faith and allegiance to the US Constitution, the army, their unit and other soldiers
- *Duty*—fulfilling their obligations
- *Respect*—treating people as they should be treated
- *Selfless service*—putting the welfare of the nation, the army, and subordinates before their own
- *Honor*—living up to army values
- *Integrity*—doing what's right, legally and morally

- *Personal courage*—facing fear, danger, or adversity (physical or moral)[1]

---

These seven values are the beginnings of the foundation of all they will learn and become during their time in military service. These values are the essence of who a soldier is—the characteristics that define them as soldiers.

In this section of your field manual you are going to learn what comprises the foundation of the soldier of God's army. Your spiritual operations guidebook—God's Word—gives clear and compelling principles that you must internalize as your own. As a good Christian soldier you must learn to live out the characteristics that God says define the soldier in His army.

Like with the United States Army, there are seven core spiritual values that define the soldier in God's army. You will find these in 2 Timothy 2:1–7:

> So you, my son, be strong (strengthened inwardly) in the grace (spiritual blessing) that is [to be found only] in Christ Jesus. And the [instructions] which you have heard from me along with many witnesses, transmit and entrust [as a deposit] to reliable and faithful men who will be competent and qualified to teach others also. Take [with me] your share of the hardships and suffering [which you are called to endure] as a good (first-class) soldier of Christ Jesus. No soldier when in service gets entangled in the enterprises of [civilian] life; his aim is to satisfy and please the one who enlisted him. And if anyone enters competitive games, he is not crowned unless he competes lawfully (fairly, according to the rules laid down). [It is] the hard-working farmer [who labors to produce] who must be the first partaker of the fruits. Think over these things I am saying [understand them and grasp their application], for the Lord will grant you full insight and understanding in everything.

These seven core spiritual values are:

- *Spiritual strength*—It is the spiritual blessing of the grace of Christ Jesus dwelling within you that strengthens you.
- *Obedience*—You must learn to listen carefully to the instructions your Commander, Jesus Christ, gives to you and obey them implicitly.
- *Competency to teach others*—You are being trained to be a leader of others; you must become competent and qualified to pass on the Commander's instructions to others.
- *Sharing in the suffering of others*—Your service as a soldier of Jesus Christ is directed toward others, and you must always carry your share of hardship and suffering.
- *Separated from the entanglements of civilian life*—You must be completely separated from the world and its sinful entanglements.
- *Striving for excellence*—Just as an athlete trains to enter athletic competitions—and win—the soldier of Jesus Christ strives and trains to exhibit spiritual excellence in all he or she does.
- *Producer of spiritual fruit*—You must not only labor to see the fruit of the gospel imparted to others, but also you must first exhibit good fruit in your own life. The spiritual fruit of the soldier of God includes love, joy, peace, patience, kindness, goodness, faithfulness, gentleness, and self-control.

There will be many other important principles and characteristics that you will learn as you continue reading this field manual. But your foundation begins with the establishment of these core values. Be determined that your life will be marked by the imprint of each of these values upon your spirit.

## The Keys of a Strong Foundation

*Spiritual Boot Camp* will introduce you to the life of God's soldier. It will teach you the characteristics of a good soldier, the requirements and obligations of a good soldier, and the benefits and rewards for being a good soldier. These are all foundational principles. It will be important for you to remember that a foundation is just that—the foundation of something bigger.

It would serve no purpose for a building contractor to dig and build a strong foundation for a building and then make a decision not to go on and erect the entire building. Just so, you must continue to build yourself as the man or woman of God you were created to be. If your foundation remains strong, you will be able to move into the full revelation of the destiny God birthed within you. Guard your foundation. Keep it pure and strong. Don't allow anything to deter you from "being all you can be" in Christ.

There are important qualities you must add to your foundation of the seven spiritual core values. This section provides you a list of some of these qualities. They will require a radical determination from you to commit to developing each of these key foundational elements in your spirit as you continue to grow in your commitment to God's army. These key qualities are:

---

1. *Determination*—firmness in purpose because of a resolve in Christ
2. *Backbone*—the ability to stand under the greatest persecution and pressure
3. *High morale*—being in high praise and having the spirit of a cheerleader to encourage yourself and others in the Lord
4. *Root in morality*—understanding and exhibiting the ability to walk in the difference between good and evil
5. *Courage*—no fear

6. *Devotedness*—immeasurable dedication to the cause
7. *Tenacity*—the ability to retain and hold on to what is true
8. *Persistence*—to insist on what is right
9. *Resolve*—a formal resolution that the things pertaining to God are settled in your heart without any ifs, ands, or buts
10. *An unrelenting mind-set*—a mind to never ease up or give up concerning the matters of the kingdom
11. *A spirit of violence*—being combat ready at all times and ready to come against every antagonistic force or opposition against your position in God
12. *A submitted will*—to be dead to personal wants and opinions and totally surrendered to the Word and will of God
13. *A revelation of the government of God*—allowing an exchange to take place in your life where the things of the kingdoms of this world do not take precedent over the things of the kingdom of God

---

These qualities will begin your move forward in God's army. Be determined that nothing will hinder your forward movement. First Corinthians 9:24 tells us to run (*trecho,* moving at a constant continuous pace) that we may obtain the prize. This requires focus and complete attention on what is ahead. We must keep our eyes on the prize. Jesus is the author and finisher of our faith. The enemy sends assignments of *unawares* (*pareisduno*, Jude 4). These are things that creep into our lives to settle into our environment without notice. If you allow them, they will grow up with you in your walk with God unnoticed and could eventually deter you from becoming all that God wants you to be.

Make 2 Timothy 4:7 your main spiritual goal in life...to finish the course that God places ahead of you. Paul did whatever it took to complete his assignment. He was not stuck in his ways. His strategies for completing the course included:

---

- Taking an outside job to support his ministry (Acts 18:3)
- Becoming a Jew in his approach to unbelieving Jews in order to win them to Christ (1 Cor. 9:20)
- Becoming as one under the Law to win those under the Law (1 Cor. 9:21)
- Becoming all things to men to win some to the Lord

---

Paul was determined to be the kind of spiritual soldier for God who would be victorious in fulfilling his mission of bringing others into the kingdom of God. Follow his pattern, and diligently pursue the mission God has placed before you.

Do not allow the enemy to creep in unawares and destroy your spiritual foundation. In a later chapter I will be sharing a prophetic word my church received on December 15, 2011, and the importance it carried for that season. The prophetic word included a warning to be aware of "the things that would eat away at our foundation."

During the time of this word we had a tent put over the building for the treatment of termites. God related the covering of the tent to the spiritual covering over the church. While covered, a pesticide was released to kill the bugs that would eat away at the foundation of the building. A spiritual covering is like a pesticide that eats away at the canker that is assigned to destroy our spiritual foundation. After getting rid of the bugs, we had to put reinforcements onto the main pillars of the building. In 2012 getting under the covering of the government of God will reinforce the pillars that the enemy has been gnawing at for many years. Just when it looks as though everything is about to collapse, God is releasing reinforcement. We will be reinforced:

- Financially
- In our relationships
- In our ministries
- In our family affairs
- In our mental and spiritual health

The soldier in God's army must continually be reinforced at the foundation of his or her spiritual life in order to avoid the effects of the enemy's attempts to undermine the foundation. In Revelation 3:1–6 our operations guidebook gives a powerful example of this undermining:

> And to the angel (messenger) of the assembly (church) in Sardis write: These are the words of Him Who has the seven Spirits of God [the sevenfold Holy Spirit] and the seven stars: I know your record and what you are doing; you are supposed to be alive, but [in reality] you are dead. Rouse yourselves and keep awake, and strengthen and invigorate what remains and is on the point of dying; for I have not found a thing that you have done [any work of yours] meeting the requirements of My God or perfect in His sight. So call to mind the lessons you received and heard; continually lay them to heart and obey them, and repent. In case you will not rouse yourselves and keep awake and watch, I will come upon you like a thief, and you will not know or suspect at what hour I will come.
>
> Yet you still have a few [persons'] names in Sardis who have not soiled their clothes, and they shall walk with Me in white, because they are worthy and deserving. Thus shall he who conquers (is victorious) be clad in white garments, and I will not erase or blot out his name from the Book of Life; I will acknowledge him [as Mine] and I will confess his name

> openly before My Father and before His angels. He who is able to hear, let him listen to and heed what the [Holy] Spirit says to the assemblies (churches).

Based on this passage of Scripture, I have noted the following keys that pertain to a strong foundation and how to maintain it:

---

1. God keeps a record of what we do.
2. God knows the actual state that we are in from the inside out.
3. God is calling the church out of the spirit of slumber to be awake, alert, and on call, which is the mandate for the end-time soldier.
4. We must be strengthened and invigorated (filled with energy and zeal to accomplish the assignment at hand) in what we have before it dies out.
5. We must make sure that the works that we do meet God's requirements and not man's; there is a way that seems right to a man, but the end of it is death. God said that the works He found were not perfect (*pleroo*—not complete, not furnished, not equipped, below standard, unaccomplished, and imperfect according to His will).
6. God demands that we recall the lessons we have learned. If we do not use what we have, we will lose it. We must lay these things to heart and obey them.
7. We must repent for intentional disobedience. It is a sin to know to do right and not do it.
8. If we continue to be slothful in the things of God, He will come like a thief in the night. He will come when we least expect Him.
9. We must be dressed spiritually correct. Our clothes cannot be soiled, and we must walk with God in personal purity. Only the victorious will be clad in white (purity).

10. The spirit of *nikaho* (victory) is upon the obedient. Despite the obstacles put before us in life, it causes us to prevail and win in the end.
11. Our names will not be erased from the Book of Life. Jesus will acknowledge us as His and will confess our names openly before God and His angels.

---

## Maintaining a Spiritual Posture

Since becoming an elected official and having the opportunity to participate in meetings governed by parliamentary procedures, I have come to understand the importance of *maintaining the right posture*. Being in place and maintaining the right position have everything to do with making the right decisions. When I think of spiritual posture, I think of the military commands we received daily as we operated as a group of soldiers. Commands had to be set in place so that a group filled with different kinds of people could move in synchronization with the orders given. I have listed a few of these orders that may be beneficial in understanding spiritual discipline of discipleship.

---

1. *Attention.* This is given to call the group to order. It requires that the soldier stand straight up and down, arms to the side, with eyes forward and ears to hear what the person in charge is saying.

   *Spiritual significance:* God wants to have our attention. He cannot give us commands and orders while we are distracted by things in life. He is calling the church at large to spiritual attention.

2. *Parade rest.* This command is given only from the position of attention. It is a more relaxed position than *attention* but still requires silence and no movement. The soldier puts both hands in the small of his back with his elbows sticking out on both sides, parallel to the ground. This is a position where instruction is given.

   *Spiritual significance:* God wants us to be comfortable with His presence yet be aware of His awesomeness and prepared to take orders and obey His orders at any cost.

3. *At ease.* This position is usually given to give soldiers a break. They can talk, socialize, and so forth as long as they stay in formation.

   *Spiritual significance:* God wants us to live an abundant life as long as we stay in place within *the formation of the Lord.*

4. *Eyes right.* This command is usually given during parades or ceremonies. The entire group is commanded to turn their eyes (to the right) toward a dignitary while they are marching.

   *Spiritual significance:* We must keep our eyes on Jesus, who is the author and finisher of our faith. One day every eye will see Him and every tongue will confess that He is Lord when the ultimate *eyes right* command is called.

5. *Dress right dress.* This command is used to make sure that a squad, unit, or platoon is lined up properly. Soldiers align themselves with other soldiers next to them so that they can be uniform and in order.

   *Spiritual significance:* The lines of the Spirit are falling upon us in sweet and agreeable places. As these lines fall on us as individuals, we must line up fitly joined together in the unity of faith for the end-time harvest.

6. *Marking time.* To march in place, not moving forward but still maintaining the cadence of the march.

   *Spiritual significance:* Those who wait on the Lord will not be ashamed. As we wait, though we are not moving ahead of God, we are doing what we know to do and not being idle.

7. *Double time.* To escalate the pace from a marching pace to a faster pace (double the pace). This pace is slower than a usual running pace but faster than a march. The purpose is to pick up momentum.

   *Spiritual significance:* There is a double portion for those who will move out in a double-time anointing. We must keep up with the momentum and cadence of God for the hour that we are in. Elijah told

Elisha that if he kept up with him and saw him when he was caught up to heaven, he would receive the double portion.

8. *March.* A command given to move two or more soldiers from one place to another in order.

   *Spiritual significance:* God told the children of Israel to move forward. He gave them their marching orders. Our marching orders are to move forward and to never go back.

---

As we close this chapter, it is important that you understand the terms *preparatory command* and *command of execution.* The preparatory command gets the attention of the soldiers to let them know that an order is being given; for example, the preparatory command "Group!" lets the group know that an order is about to be given. The order could be "Attention." "Group" is the preparatory command and "Attention" is the command of execution, which means to execute what is ordered.

And last but not least, a person cannot prepare or execute a command without being present or in place. As soldiers of the Lord we must be careful not to be AWOL (absent without leave). When God gives an order, we must be in place to obey. God must be able to put His finger on us at all times. When Adam and Eve fell into sin, God had to ask, "Where are you?" This is a question we never want the Lord to have to ask us. We must take an aggressive posture in God and stay in place.

# Chapter 4

## BE DISCIPLINED AND SHARP

Boot camp changes a man or woman into a soldier. The eight weeks that I spent in basic training changed everything I thought I knew about life. The most important thing I received during my transition from civilian to soldier was discipline.

Joining the military was a huge step for me—but one that I knew was my only way out of the chaos of drug addiction and street living. I am convinced that if I had not joined the army, I would have been a casualty of life like most of the people I hung out with. Most of the people I knew from my past are dead, in mental institutions, incarcerated, infected with AIDS, or walking around the streets out of their mind.

It is a miracle that I passed the drug test at the military entrance processing (MEP) station, but God knew that I would not have lasted much longer on the streets. I had to make it out. I will never forget the sergeant at the MEP station who did a final interview for my induction. He asked me if I had ever used drugs, and I told him that I had. He asked me when was the last time I used drugs and what kind. I told him that I had gotten high the night before on cocaine. He was so shocked at my frankness, but he still allowed me to enlist. He must have had a gut feeling about me, because I never used drugs again.

The army provided the discipline that I needed. I needed discipline and structure in my life, and that is just what Uncle Sam provided. I had just gotten off track. I became a world-class athlete who was disciplined and focused. The army has a phrase, "Be All That You Can Be!" I can take this saying to another level. For anyone who really wants to be something in life, the army will teach you *who you are*, and it starts with basic training. I think that a military boot camp, with the right structure and with leaders who have a passion to bring the best out of people, is the answer for the rehabilitation of people who have gotten on the wrong road in life.

It took the drill sergeants seven weeks to break me. People on the wrong track must be broken. That spirit of rebellion must be confronted and sternly dealt with. I believe that boot camps are not just needed for the people who have become criminally minded but also for individuals who have no order, discipline, or submission to authority in their lives. I was the poster child for both cases.

I had a big nicotine habit when I went into basic training. The rule of thumb was that a trainee could smoke only when he or she was given permission. In other words, smoking was a privilege! This simply did not compute in my mind. I smoked in the stairwell in the barracks at 2:00 and 3:00 A.M. before the other trainees got up. I even smoked in the bathroom on the fire range behind the ammunition shed. At the risk of everyone's life, I was determined those drill sergeants would not tell me when I could smoke. In my mind, I was a grown woman!

One time another trainee told the drill sergeants that I was in the bathroom smoking on the fire range. The bathroom was behind the ammunition shed at the bottom of a hill. The platoon was shooting at the top of the hill. When I came out of the bathroom, three furious drill sergeants were running down the hill telling me to get up against the wall of the bathroom. They pushed my face to the wall with my arms in the air, touching the wall. The senior drill sergeant was a big, dark-skinned man, and he was yelling at the top of his voice, "You're going to jail this time, Private!" They stood around me yelling like I had killed someone. They got right in my ear and said the same thing over and over again: "Private, you're going to jail!" I was thinking that at least in jail I could smoke. The pressure of fighting against the goad in basic training made me only wish that I could go back to the streets. Despite this, something on the inside of me told me that I would die if I did.

One particular drill sergeant literally hated my guts. I had a lot of hair on my head and no time to comb it. He would get in my face, nose to nose, and curse me out every day. The crazy thing was that I would yell back at him. I was not afraid of him. His position and authority over me only fed my demons and made me more rebellious. I would literally stand toe to toe with this drill sergeant, and we would exchange words: "You hit me first!" "No, you hit me first!" This guy made my life a living nightmare, one that had become personal.

One day another trainee came to me and told me she knew how I could get the pressure off of me. I could not believe when she told me that some of the trainees were having midnight rendezvous with a few of the drill sergeants, and my guy was one of them. Instead of bowing to the easy way out, I decided to set this drill sergeant up. I went as far as to make an appointment with the company commander, but something on the inside of me could not do it. About five years ago I sat on a plane with that same drill sergeant. I told him who I was, and he remembered me. He was retired and seemed to be really laid back. I felt like it was my confirmation that I was not supposed to take matters into my own hands. I could see the guilt in his eyes as I told him about all that I had accomplished since boot camp.

Boot camp is all about discipline, discipline, discipline! To have discipline, you must learn how to be a disciple—you must learn how to follow. During those seven weeks of fighting the system, my rebellious actions included:

---

- Leaving my pup tent in the training field in the wee hours of the morning to finding a corner (to sleep in) in the tent of ten drill sergeants who were sleeping (It was not a pretty sight when they woke up.)

- Never running with the platoon during physical training as I was instructed to do
- Never cleaning the common areas with the other sixty women in my bay
- Bullying other female trainees

---

It just seemed like I could not do what I was told because I was so set in my ways. I had been smoking and going to clubs since I was fourteen years old. Submission to anyone was not a part of my plan. My plans changed when a drill sergeant found me sleeping on fire guard duty and informed me that I was going to be recycled. I panicked. "Recycled, what does that mean?" The reality hit me as he explained to me that I would not be put out of the military but would start boot camp over from week one. I was terrified at the idea. I started crying, and the drill sergeant felt sorry for me and told me what to do. He told me to submit and get with the program. I was ready to cry "Uncle!" I gave in to my temper, my pride, and anything else that I had left. I knew that a physical training (PT) test was scheduled for the next morning, and I had convinced a doctor to put a fake cast on my leg to get me out of running with the platoon. That night I chiseled off the cast on my leg. I showed up at the PT test and received a score of 300, a perfect physical fitness score. I went back to the barracks and grabbed the buffer to do the floors. I mopped floors, dusted the barracks, cleaned the toilets, and did anything I could to let the drill sergeants know I had learned my lesson. I wanted to become a soldier in the one week left in my boot camp experience, not in nine weeks, which would include *eight more weeks of boot camp*!

My senior drill sergeant apologized to me for not recognizing my leadership skills from the day I got off the cattle truck. He said, "I missed it. If I would have made you my platoon leader, things would have been easier for everyone." I graduated with the understanding that if I wanted to be a soldier, I would always be accountable to someone. Accountability was never a part of my life before this time. I was finally relieved that I had to answer to someone besides myself. It is pretty hard having the last say in your life.

The discipline that I received as a soldier in the natural army prepared me to be a trooper for the Lord. After basic training I never received lower than a score of 300 on my PT test. I became the fastest female in the armed forces and make rank at a supernatural pace.

My senior drill sergeant took back all the negative words that he had said about me. He concluded that I would do well in the military, and I did. I was broken, and my mind was renewed.

The scripture that reminds me of my boot camp experience is Romans 12:1–2:

> I appeal to you therefore, brethren, and beg of you in view of [all] the mercies of God, to make a decisive dedication of your bodies [presenting all your members and faculties] as a living sacrifice, holy (devoted, consecrated) and well pleasing to God, which is your reasonable (rational, intelligent) service and spiritual worship. Do not be conformed to this world (this age), [fashioned after and adapted to its external, superficial customs], but be transformed (changed) by the [entire] renewal of your mind [by its new ideals and its new attitude], so that you may prove [for yourselves] what is the good and acceptable and perfect will of God, even the thing which is good and acceptable and perfect [in His sight for you].

## Be Renewed—Mind and Body

Yes, my mind was renewed, but my body had to follow. I could not just think like a soldier; I had to look like one. Just as I have learned to present my body as a living sacrifice as a believer, I also had to present myself as a sharp soldier. A part of being a soldier is looking the part. Soldiers who do not present themselves according to the standard of the army are called *rag-bag* soldiers. Not only does negative conduct identify a rag-bag soldier, but an improper appearance does also. The standard set for a soldier's duty appearance includes:

- Standard haircuts and hairstyles for men and women
- A nicely pressed uniform
- Freshly shined boots
- Rank and other accessories on the uniform in place

When I started understanding how important it was to be a disciplined soldier, I desired to be sharp. My appearance was just as important as my job performance. My uniform could stand in a corner by itself, it was starched so hard. My hat was even starched. My boots were not just cleaned and shined but spit-shined. I would burn the wax into the tips of my boots and shine them until they looked like glass. This was in no way about vanity; it was about being proud to be a soldier.

Living in the barracks instilled another level of discipline in my everyday life. Because we had periodic inspections, I formed a habit of having a floor that looked like glass, having an orderly closet, and maintaining a dust-free environment. Today these disciplines are ingrained in me. Though they are natural disciplines, they have set a pattern in my mind that affects how I do almost everything I do.

## Spiritual Boot Camp Dynamics

How does all of this relate to being in a spiritual boot camp? When we come into the things of God, we make the transition from the world to the kingdom. Our mind must be continually renewed by the Word of God. At the same time, what is on the inside of us must be seen by others. Our transformation must not be kept a secret. We must be disciplined and sharp for the Lord. We should be proud to be in the Lord's army. We cannot be ashamed of the gospel of Jesus Christ. Every day we need to be dressed for battle, and our areas of operation (AOs) should be "dress right dress" and in order. Wherever there is clutter and confusion, we can never be combat ready.

I would not trade my experience in basic training for anything in the world. I want your experience through this field manual of spiritual boot camp to be the same. I pray that God will allow you to get rid of old bad habits in your life to acquire new positive ones. I have found that it usually takes four to eight weeks to break old habits. My life-changing experience was seven weeks in the United States Army. It prepared me for the Lord's army. Your experience may not be in the United States Army, but I believe that God has a tailor-made spiritual situation for you. Let's pray:

> *Father, I pray for this reader, in the name of Jesus. I pray that You would cause the natural to collide with the Spirit realm to lay a foundation for discipline. I pray for a strong consistent prayer life, a dedicated study discipline in the Word, and a time of consecration for praise and worship. I break every curse of laziness, sleepiness, or distraction. I decree and declare a sharpness that will cut away anything that would cause dullness and a lack of cutting-edge response. Remove every person, place, or thing that is a buffer preventing change. Establish relationships that are prosperous to the calling of God. I release the zeal of the Lord and the fervor of the Holy Spirit so that the work you have begun will be a finished work. Amen.*

## Chapter 5

# THE GREATEST GIFT—LOVE

★★★★★

WHEN ENGAGED IN warfare, we must remember that an army with *solo soldiers* or *lone rangers* will fail. Though great warriors may be highlighted, the strength of a good army is the ability for soldiers to be comrades. In other words, they must look out for and respect each other. With all the talent and skill soldiers may have, care for their fellow trench buddy is a must. The Bible makes reference to having gifts with no love. God says it is like a loud screeching musical sound that is far off-key. Because I have been in a real war situation during Operation Desert Storm, I understand compassion for the man or woman you are working with every day, knowing that he or she may not live to see the next day.

I have been in spiritual warfare and deliverance ministry for years. I have learned to appreciate the variety of God. He uses all kinds of people in all kinds of ways. Even in the church God has given different gifts to men that manifest themselves in different administrations. I am proud to be a part of the end-time apostolic move of God. My soul gets stirred when I see the miracles of God, and I am especially motivated when God uses gifted people to minister to the nations. Despite all of this, I cannot ignore how some gifted people have brought a reproach on the ministries of the Lord. God has allowed the gifts and the callings that He has given to us to remain in our lives even if we get off track. His gifts are irrevocable (Rom. 11:29).

We must come to the realization that when one saint falls, it affects the entire body. As a soldier in God's army, you must learn to support your fellow spiritual soldiers and pray for them, especially in times like these. Our witness as believers is so important in the last days. How do we start supporting others? First we must pray for all believers and especially those on the front lines. If you are a woman, it is especially important to pray for women in ministry. The devil hates women, and he has a deep-seated hatred for women on the front lines of ministry.

It is the mercy and grace of God that keep reproaches off our lives and ministries. I do all that I know to do to serve the Lord faithfully, but the traps of the enemy are very real. I do not believe that most leaders or laypeople plan on getting in situations that bring a reproach to the gospel of Jesus Christ. The Bible says if it were possible, even the elect would be deceived (Matt. 24:24). I have been preaching for years that we must walk out our salvation in fear and trembling. I have seen that so many times when people think more of themselves than they ought to, they fall prey to the traps of the enemy. I am confident in my deliverance, but I am careful to never boast about what I *would not do*. A prideful person is doomed to fall into the things he or she is prideful about. It is only by the mercy and the grace of God that we are free indeed. Our liberty is not by our power to keep ourselves—it is by God's power to keep us. Many people fall into sin because they attempt to keep themselves. I thank God for keeping me! As you are reading this teaching, you should take the time to thank God for keeping you.

Because the gifts and callings of God are irrevocable, we must check out our love walk. We have to be careful that we do not get so caught up in our gifts that we lose our relationship with God. This is what happened to the priests in Ezekiel 44. They fell into sin, but God allowed them to stay in their positions over the people. They continued to keep charge of the temple, but God removed them from their positions in Him. They *could no longer be close to God!* All believers should fear this curse—having a great ministry to people but never being able to come close to God.

The Lord has given us a sure way to keep our ministries to the people and maintain a healthy relationship with Him. He wants us to make sure that we have *the greatest gift of all.* There are many great spiritual gifts. I am sure that many would say that prophetic power is the greatest gift. The ability to understand all the secret truths and mysteries in our operations guidebook, God's Word, would be at the top of the list for many. For others, moving mountains and raising the dead are the greatest gifts. Though all these gifts are great and truly to be desired, they do not compare to the greatest gift of all, *which is love.* We can have all the things I mentioned above and still be nothing in the eyes of God if we do not have love. Without love people can still call you great and desire your presence, but you will not be able to abide in the presence of the Lord.

For additional confirmation of the importance of the gift of love, read "Section 5-1: The Greatest Gift—Love: The Importance of Love" in Appendix A.

## Abide in Faith, Hope, and Love

The Word of the Lord commands us to abide in faith, hope, and love. *Faith* is the conviction and belief respecting man's relationship to God and divine things. *Hope* is the joyful, confident expectation of eternal salvation. Finally, *love* is true affection for God and man growing out of God's love for (and in) us. Faith, hope, and love are the threefold cord for prosperity in our spiritual lives. Though we need all of them, God puts a priority on LOVE! The Book of Ephesians talks about being rooted and grounded in love (Eph. 3:17). When something is grounded in a thing, that element is its foundation.

For example, electric wires run throughout a city so that city has electrical power in its homes. Those wires must be grounded. If the wires are not grounded, the electricity can run wild. When we are grounded in love, it is love that directs the focus of the gifts and callings of God to fulfill God's purpose and bless His people. Our ministries will be set ablaze by the fire (power) of the Lord and not loosed like a wild fire that destroys everything it comes into contact with.

To be *rooted* means "to get your source from." When love is your foundation and your source, you can never be disconnected from God. God is your source. Jesus is supposed to be the center of your joy. True love is always accompanied with joy. It is difficult to believe that a person loves a thing when the person seems to be miserable with that thing. It is sad to see many people who claim to love the Lord but at the same time appear miserable serving Him.

Love is the root and the source of our faith. It is the gas we need to keep our spiritual engines running. It is the only thing that will help us to fight the "good fight of faith" (1 Tim. 6:12). Many people buy my books and attend my conferences because they want to know more about spiritual warfare. This chapter on the importance of love will give balance and help warfare-minded soldiers to fight the good fight of faith without becoming weary in well-doing. By the time you finish this lesson, you will understand *the warfare of love*. When the enemy challenges your faith, tries to bring a reproach on your ministry, and attacks your mind, the love of God is a safe haven for you to abide in and from which to come out victorious.

## Called to Love

The number one question that people ask around the world is, "How do I know what I am called to do for the Lord?" I can easily begin to answer that question, but only the Lord can finish it. *The first calling of every believer is to walk in love*. This is the prerequisite for ministry. As you walk in love, you will be on the road to fulfilling the destiny of your high calling.

God loved the world so much that He sent His Son, Jesus, to die for our sins. Ministry is rooted in compassion and love. God's heart burns for us to experience the fullness of life. Jesus came to fulfill that desire. I do not understand ministers who preach and teach but do not even like people. The bottom line in ministry is that we must love people—the good, the bad, and the ugly.

I have heard ministers express their ill feelings toward having to deal with the problems that people have. My advice to any minister who does not have the patience and compassion to deal with messed-up people is for them to get another occupation. Jesus came for messed-up people, and His gospel is tailor-made for the good, the bad, and the ugly.

In Ephesians 4:1 Paul warned the people to walk worthy of the vocation to which they were called. Ministry is not a vacation—IT IS A JOB! Those who are looking to be driven around in limousines, vacation in five-star hotels, and have servants to attend to their needs will be highly disappointed and most likely unfulfilled. The ministry of Jesus Christ is to be carried out with special instruction from God. These instructions keep the unity of the Spirit. Before we attain unity of faith, we must tap into the unity of the Spirit.

Just as the United States Army requires teamwork and ultimate cooperation from its soldiers, our Commander, God, requires the soldiers in His army to work together as a team to build His kingdom. The fourth chapter of Ephesians gives us important principles for learning to do this. Continue your study on the importance of love by studying "Section 5-2: The Greatest Gift—Love: The Principles of the Unity of Love" in Appendix A.

## Chapter 6

# DEVELOP GOOD COMMON SENSE

After a long night at a city council meeting, one of the committee chairmen pulled me off and said, "I really want to work with you on some procedural things because you have unusually good *common sense*." This stayed in my spirit for weeks, and I began to think on how the church needs good common sense. Believers can sometimes be so spiritually minded that they cannot relate to the common things of the world. We are not of the world, but we must be able to relate to the world to win them. A perfect example is the passage of Scripture in Luke 16:8–13:

> And [his] master praised the dishonest (unjust) manager for acting shrewdly and prudently; for the sons of this age are shrewder and more prudent and wiser in [relation to] their own generation [to their own age and kind] than are the sons of light. And I tell you, make friends for yourselves by means of unrighteous mammon (deceitful riches, money, possessions), so that when it fails, they [those you have favored] may receive and welcome you into the everlasting habitations (dwellings). He who is faithful in a very little [thing] is faithful also in much, and he who is dishonest and unjust in a very little [thing] is dishonest and unjust also in much. Therefore if you have not been faithful in the [case of] unrighteous mammon (deceitful riches, money, possessions), who will entrust to you the true riches? And if you have not proved

> faithful in that which belongs to another [whether God or man], who will give you that which is your own [that is, the true riches]? No servant is able to serve two masters; for either he will hate the one and love the other, or he will stand by and be devoted to the one and despise the other. You cannot serve God and mammon (riches, or anything in which you trust and on which you rely).

In this story the master was dealing with a dishonest manager of his affairs. The key point that we should get out of this lesson is that when the man had done wrong, he went out of his way to *make it right.* God does not expect for us to be perfect, but He does want us to have the ability to make it right when we fall short. The Bible is full of men and women of God who had to make things right.

The unjust steward was clearly guilty, but he did not *make excuses*; he made it right! Though he was wrong in the management of the master's affairs, he was commended. The Lord said that the children of the world are in their generation wiser than the children of light (v. 8). This is a powerful statement! The Lord went on to say that we should make friends of unrighteous mammon so that when we fail, they may receive us into everlasting habitation (v. 9). A carnally minded person could easily think that the Lord was asking us to compromise, but this is not the case. The Lord was saying that we have to learn how to operate in the world in which He has called His people to reign and have dominion.

While we have been building megaministries and filling pews, the children of the world have been making laws and putting institutions in place to control the thinking of our children. As believers we have a right to impart to a generation that has our values. *WE* have fallen short in this. Religious spirits perpetrate to distract and defraud us in the separating of ourselves into church cubicles while the world goes on without us. Believers are called to get involved in government, professional athletics, Hollywood, and other local and national affairs that affect our well-being.

The Lord makes the statement that if we are faithful in that which is least, He will anoint us to rule over much. He goes on to say that if we are not faithful in unrighteous mammon, who will commit us to the true riches? My interpretation of what God is saying is that we should not despise small beginnings but be faithful in dealing with them. We also should not shun positions, jobs, or assignment in the things of the world.

All believers are not called to work in the ministry. Do not get me wrong; working in the ministry is the greatest honor of all, but we live in the world. God did not set His kingdom outside of the world but in the midst of it. We are called to be the light of the world and the salt of the earth.

Some people tripped out when I ran for city council in my city, but after almost ninety-three thousand votes in a campaign of just six to eight weeks, they stopped tripping! God takes the foolish things to confound those who think they have it figured out.

The unjust steward is the poster child for common sense. He could not depend on a degree or even people of influence he knew. He had to think fast and be quick on his feet, or he was finished. He did several things to regain favor with his master:

---

1. He had the right attitude when his master addressed him.
2. He took responsibility and was accountable for what he had done.
3. He did not try to make the situation easier for himself by making excuses.
4. He offered an answer to the problem he had caused.
5. He made it happen.

---

The unjust steward is a type of a person of the world. Could you imagine a believer who may have gotten into the same situation?

Just because people are saved does not mean they do right. What if a believer would have quoted scriptures to try to cover his or her error, saying things like:

---

- "God knows my heart."
- "We all fall short of His glory."
- "God's mercy and grace are sufficient."

---

No! No! No! These passages are not the answer. The answer is making right to the best of your ability what you have made wrong. Some people attempt to *live in the Bible* when we are called to have the Word of God in our hearts to help us to *live in the world.* We cannot be so heavenly minded that we are no earthly good. There is not a church building large enough for the harvest that God wants. He wants us to be earthly good. This is the greatest tool of evangelism. We must have a ministry of common sense to common people.

I was invited to a union ball as a city council representative. People were drinking and partying and doing what the world does. There were about thirty-five hundred people at the event, and I was wondering how the city paid for drinks for so many people. I was told that coupons were placed in the envelopes with the tickets for a limited amount of free drinks. I did not get any coupons for drinks with my tickets. Unfortunately, this would not have been the case with all pastors. Though I am an elected official, they understood that I am a woman of God first. This will never change. I was relieved in my spirit that the leaders of this event respected the fact that I was in the situation but not "of it."

The ultimate test of holiness and salvation is to have the ability to live and operate in a world system that is ruled by the dictates of the flesh and under a demonic regime. Satan is the god of this world. Don't you ever forget it!

Matthew 11:19 says that people described Jesus as a drunk, glutton, and a friend of publicans and sinners. Jesus did not keep His ministry in the synagogue. He visited often, but His ministry was to the world. He is the Son of Man who came to save those who were lost.

Jeremiah gives an interesting account of a group of God's people. The King James Version calls them "sottish children," as Jeremiah stated, "They are sottish children, and they have none understanding: they are wise to do evil, but to do good they have no knowledge" (Jer. 4:22, KJV). The key words in this passage are:

---

- *Understanding* (*biyn*)—to have no discernment and to not be cunning; to have no feeling as to what was going on, to be uninformed and uninstructed; to have no prudence, perception, or skill concerning the matter; to be unable to think or do wisely when the situation arose
- *Knowledge* (*yada*)—acquaintance; acknowledgement; awareness; cunning; familiar friend; respect; skill; wit; surety

---

The word *sottish* means to be silly and foolish. This term is mentioned in the Bible once. Jeremiah was saying that this was a group of God's people who were not relevant. As believers we must be holy, but God is also calling us to be relevant. Yes, the world will hate us, but there will be people we will be able to relate to, and they will relate to us and be saved. Without relationships we cannot win souls. God will put us in positions or places so that we can acquire relationships that will cause people to want what we have. These relationships are not to judge people or to push Jesus down their throats. They are to bring Jesus to places and platforms so that people can at least imagine what God is like and to let our light shine.

## Daniel—God's Soldier in a Wicked World

The first chapter of Daniel explains what I am saying well. Daniel and the Hebrew boys had a résumé that caused them to outshine the other young boys in Babylon.

---

- They were without blemish.
- They were well favored in appearance.
- They were skillful in all wisdom.
- They were cunning in knowledge.
- They had great understanding of science.
- They were competent to stand and serve in the king's palace.
- They had the ability to teach the literature and language of the Chaldeans.

---

Wow, these kids had it going on. They were saved, sanctified, and RELEVANT! The key was that they did not partake of the king's portion. And even in not partaking of the king's portion, they requested permission to refrain from partaking with respect to the ruling authorities who governed over them.

The most interesting thing I found in this study was the fact that they knew the literature and language of the Chaldeans well enough to teach it. This reminds me of a big problem in the church. Church folk do not understand the language of the world and those who operate on the other side. I have had so many people who attend church faithfully tell me that they believe in God but do not believe in the devil. This is a blatant disrespect for the Word of God. Who do they think they are to defy the Holy Scriptures? If the Bible says there is a devil…HE EXISTS! The sad thing is that he controls and exists more forcefully in the lives of those who do not believe he exists. Most believers do not know warfare literature or language. They do not even know that witches exist. God says that His people perish for a lack of knowledge (Hos. 4:6). Some things are common sense. If there is a heaven... there is a hell. And if there is a God... there is a devil.

## Moses and Jethro

I cannot close out my teaching on common sense without talking about the story of Moses and his father-in-law, Jethro. This example seals the deal on common sense. In Exodus 3 Moses had an encounter with the burning bush while he was at Jethro's house. Jethro was serving idol gods, and he was a heathen. As religious minds would have it, experiencing the burning bush close to the synagogue or some place of religious notoriety would have been ideal. Well, God does not operate like that. After his encounter with the Most High, Moses asked his heathen father-in-law's permission to go back to Egypt. Moses had been with God, yet he still extended common courtesy toward Jethro.

Jethro later went to visit Moses in the wilderness while Moses was leading God's people. When Jethro saw the burden of the counsel that Moses had to give to so many people, he told him to train elders to support him. Jethro brought it to Moses's attention that he would not last long based on his solo efforts to administer counseling to all the people.

Based on this, I can feel safe in saying that the reason we have elders in the church was not because of chief priests or prophets but because of a man with good common sense, Jethro. Religiously speaking, some would argue that Jethro was giving ungodly counsel because of his status. The truth of the matter is that God uses whom He chooses, and it is usually not the same people whom men would choose. Moses also had the common sense to follow the discernment of a natural elder in his life who had his best interests in mind.

## Nehemiah

Last but not least, Nehemiah's vision to rebuild the wall of Jerusalem is a perfect example of common sense. Nehemiah did not consult a prophet or priest for permission for his assignment; he asked the Babylonian king. The king gave Nehemiah permission, provision, and release to rebuild the walls of Jerusalem (Neh. 2:1–9).

Having the imprint of the signet ring of a heathen king gave Nehemiah safe passage through all the provinces to rebuild the walls of Jerusalem.

Matthew 10:16 says, "Behold, I am sending you out like sheep in the midst of wolves; be wary and wise as serpents, and be innocent (harmless, guileless, and without falsity) as doves." The word *wise* is *phronimos* in the Greek language, and it means:

---

- To be thoughtful
- To be discreet and cautious in character
- To have practical skills and good common sense

---

Need I say more? In spiritual warfare things will arise about which you have not necessarily read a book or attended a class. In natural combat only the soldiers with discernment and good common sense survive the battle and make it back home…*selah!*

## Getting in the Trenches of Prayer

As a soldier in God's army, you will need to develop the habit of praying principled scriptures from our operations guidebook. Understanding the principles of prayer is very important. In Sections 6-1 and 6-2 of Appendix A you will find additional study materials on the importance of common sense about the topic of prayer. Section 6-1 contains a listing of terms and prayer practices that you should be able to identify and use. Section 6-2 contains vitally important prayer principles from God's Word.

Before you move to these additional study resources, there are two very important things to note about prayer. You must know:

---

- What to pray
- How to apply the principles of prayer to your prayer efforts so that you will stay on course

---

Many people start out with the right intentions in their spiritual disciplines but get off course. The glue that keeps us in place is the will and the Word of God. Ignorance is not an excuse in the kingdom. God warns us that His people perish for a lack of knowledge (Hos. 4:6). Make a determination that you will do all that you can to become knowledgeable in the principles and instructions in our spiritual operations Guidebook—the Word of God.

## Chapter 7

# BE A WOMAN OF VALOR (VIRTUE)

THE SUBJECT OF women in authority has been a controversial topic for many years. Though we have "come a long way, baby," we still have a way to go. A principle that has really helped me in life is this: in order to walk in that which is real, *avoid the counterfeit!* This chapter touches on the topic of counterfeit virtue. Remember, everything that God has, the devil has a counterfeit.

### COUNTERFEIT VIRTUE

Most of the pictures that have been painted of the Proverbs 31 woman do not line up with that scripture. In this chapter I will address the essence of true virtue. First I would like to identify false virtue, which the world holds high in admiration concerning the role of women. The world holds New Age teachings undergirded with astrology and mythology in high esteem. Most believers do not realize that through these traditions, cultures, and teachings demon entities are worshipped. For example, there is a demon power behind every mythological god. Let's take a look at a few of them and identify what people literally pray for these false gods to provide to them:

- Aphrodite/Venus—irresistible good looks (called the goddess of love)
- Artemis/Diana—easy childbirth; success in running
- Athene/Minerva—clever strategies; domestic skills; practical wisdom
- Demeter/Ceres—fertility
- Hecate/Juno—faithfulness in marriage
- Hestia/Vesta—protection at home and hearth
- Muses—inspiration in music and poetry

These deities were worshipped and prayed to for the things listed above. Venus is popular as the goddess of love. It is no surprise that this goddess was prayed to for irresistible good looks. Today women refer to themselves as *divas*. The word *diva* is short for divination and means "female goddess." You cannot be a diva and be saved. Divas do not have true virtue!

Mythology affects our society more than we are aware. A lot of these entities are directly connected to astrological charts, which the secular world lives by. Horoscopes are published daily on the Internet and in newspapers. You would be surprised to find out how many believers follow the instructions of horoscopes to live their lives. Christians should not be involved with horoscopes. The zodiac (information in the stars) is scriptural and is noted in Job 38:32. This means that information on our lives is kept in the heavens. The lines of the Spirit fall upon us, and we have destinies that cannot be denied. This destiny is found in being seated in heavenly places with Christ Jesus, not in following stars.

When I did a study of the stars in the Old Testament, they mostly related to angels. The stars that lined up over Jael as Deborah prophesied were angelic beings according to the Hebrew translation of the word *stars*. They fought in the heavens so that the words spoken by Deborah would not fall to the ground. Even with this revelation, we must understand that our destinies are not in angels; they did not die and shed blood for us. Jesus holds that place in our lives alone!

Musicians, scientists, and artists give praise to the Muses for inspiration in their art. The Muses were said to be children of Zeus and Mnemosyne (the goddess of memory). They are:

---

- Calliope—the Muse of epic poetry
- Clio—the Muse of history
- Erato—the Muse of song
- Euterpe—the Muse of lyric poetry
- Melpomene—the Muse of tragedy
- Polyhymnia—the Muse of scared song
- Thalia—the Muse of comedy
- Terpsichore—the Muse of dance
- Urania—the Muse of astronomy

---

The issue is not if these mythological creatures exist. The importance of this study is that people believe they exist and worship and give them homage. People depend on these deities to meet their needs. God does not want us to depend on anything for our needs except Him. When people pray or even give heed to these deities, they entertain familiar spirits (demons that travel through the family bloodline) and evoke demons. True virtuous women are sensitive to counterfeit spirits that attempt to rule in our homes and even through professional arenas.

## Lilith

Isaiah 34:14 speaks of a mythological creature called Lilith. The names used in the Bible that relate to this spirit are *demon of the desert*, the *night hag*, and the *screech owl*. Lilith is a type of succubus (a demon that has sex with mortal men; see Genesis 6, which describes when demons came down and had sex with women in the earth; this is how giants were created), a spirit that usually attacks people while they are sleeping. Legend teaches that Lilith is an enemy of God that has vowed to kill babies before one year of age. This is why we bind Lilith before we pray against crib death.

Legend also says that Lilith was a demon in the garden (before Eve) that tempted Adam, and this why God said it was not good for man to be alone. Some may argue that this is not biblical truth. My position is that it is spiritual truth! There are certain things in the Bible that can only be spiritually discerned. I can confirm that the demon exists, and if it exists now, it has been here since the beginning of time.

I pray that you will not consider the things I have just mentioned from a natural point of view. The natural man or carnal mind cannot understand and will fight the things of the spirit. The women's feminist movement believes what I have said enough that Lilith is the symbol for their movement. Carnality mixed with religion has been a handicap in the church. We have quoted scriptures for so long that they have become like fables that only exist in books.

The spirit realm is very real, and the Word of the Lord can only be spiritually discerned. Witches have the upper hand on people of God in this arena. They really walk by faith and not by sight. This is the only way to tap into the supernatural and do the greater works. What they do for the devil, we should do for God...BUT GREATER—the Greater One is on the inside of us!

## The Real Deal

The Proverbs 31 woman is the real deal! She is biblically known as the virtuous woman. Ruth 3:11 says that everyone in the city *knew* Ruth as virtuous. It doesn't say that everyone in the city called her virtuous. It does say that they knew it. Most of the time the world will not admit the true virtue of a Proverbs 31 woman, but deep down on the inside they cannot help but *know it.*

Proverbs 12:4 teaches that a virtuous woman is the crown of her husband. This word *crown* is *atarah* in the Hebrew, and it comes from another Hebrew word, *atar.* It means, "to encircle for attack to protect." Along with the name of the virtuous woman going before her in her city, she is like a lioness that stands guard against predators who seek to harm her family. Because she is the crown of the husband, his kingdom will not be under surprise attack. The anointing of his crown (wife) is the radar for him and all that is his to secure his domain. He is in his place as a king because he wears his crown securely on his head. He is not insecure or intimidated by the fact that his crown is aggressive against infiltration of the home, because God made woman to be that way.

The role of the virtuous woman can be easily defined by understanding the meaning of the Hebrew word *chayil* (virtuous). It means:

---

- A force to be reckoned with whether by means or resources
- An army or band of soldiers
- Wealth, valor, strength, might, power, and substance
- Able and active
- Goods
- Trained to be war worthy; having the ability to train because she has been through training, discipline, and education

---

When I studied the meaning of a real virtuous woman, it amazed me to recognize how the roles of women have been downplayed and discredited. A virtuous woman is a force to be reckoned with because she is worthy of war. The battles that she faces opens doors for her spoils, and she gets the booty of battle through the wealth of the wicked being transferred into her possession.

Not only is the virtuous woman *able,* but she is also *active.* Her God-given ability causes her not to live her life by lip service only. She manifests what she is able to do through her labor. As a result, goods, great wealth, and substance are a part of her portion. Her ultimate portion is in her God. Her strength and might are rooted in her spirituality, yet professionalism goes before her. She is covered in beauty and girded in wisdom. She is a part of an army that terrorizes demons. She does more than carry weapons against the enemy—*she is a weapon against the enemy,* the greatest weapon God ever created against darkness. She brings fear to the counterfeit because she is *the real deal*!

## Chapter 8

# DO NOT BE WEARY IN WELL-DOING

Paul was one of the greatest soldiers in God's army in the New Testament. At the end of his ministry, he declared that he had "finished my course" (2 Tim. 4:7, KJV)! The only way to finish our course or term of duty is to avoid becoming weary in well-doing.

I have had the pleasure of working with some of the greatest soldiers in God's army. These were people whom I covered and who were a part of my ministry, but they fell off for some reason or the other. They served well and walked in the anointing of God, but they fell prey to the enemy in the midst of their good work.

Nehemiah is an example of a soldier who *did not become weary in well-doing.* While he was rebuilding the walls of Jerusalem, Sanballat and Tobiah, kings of neighboring tribes of people, asked him five times to come to meet with them. But all five times Nehemiah told Sanballat and Tobiah that he was not coming off the wall because he was "doing a great work and cannot come down" (Neh. 6:3). Most fallen soldiers fall while doing a "good work."

It is of paramount importance that as soldiers in the army of God, we finish the work we begin and maintain our good work by avoiding weariness in well-doing. Our operations guidebook is filled with important admonitions about finishing the work God gives us to do. There are three relevant scriptures that refer to not becoming weary in the work of the Lord given below for you to read and internalize in your spirit. Determine to stay the course until you have finished. Let these scriptures be like marrow to your bones to build you up in your commitment to finish your race as Paul did.

**1. Galatians 6:7–9**

In this first example you will discover that God will not allow Himself to be mocked. Those who attempt to sneer at the sincere efforts of God's soldiers will be unable to make the saints weary!

> Do not be deceived and deluded and misled; God will not allow Himself to be sneered at (scorned, disdained, or mocked by mere pretensions or professions, or by His precepts being set aside.) [He inevitably deludes himself who attempts to delude God.] For whatever a man sows, that and that only is what he will reap. For he who sows to his own flesh (lower nature, sensuality) will from the flesh reap decay and ruin and destruction, but he who sows to the Spirit will from the Spirit reap eternal life. *And let us not lose heart and grow weary and faint in acting nobly and doing right*, for in due time and at the appointed season we shall reap, if we do not loosen and relax our courage and faint.
>
> —Emphasis added

**2. 2 Thessalonians 3:10–15**

Paul warned the Thessalonica church that those who refused to work in God's army should not be given food and necessities they should be earning. He also tells the faithful soldier to refuse to associate with those who will not work. Lazy brethren who do not want to work cannot make the saints weary!

> For while we were yet with you, we gave you this rule and charge: If anyone will not work, neither let him eat. Indeed, we hear that some among you are disorderly [that they are passing their lives in idleness, neglectful of duty], being busy with other people's affairs instead of their own and doing no work. Now we charge and exhort such persons [as ministers in

> Him exhorting those] in the Lord Jesus Christ (the Messiah) that they work in quietness and earn their own food and other necessities. *And as for you, brethren, do not become weary or lose heart in doing right [but continue in well-doing without weakening].* But if anyone [in the church] refuses to obey what we say in this letter, take note of that person and do not associate with him, so that he may be ashamed. Do not regard him as an enemy, but simply admonish and warn him as [being still] a brother.
>
> —Emphasis added

**3. Jeremiah 12:5–6**

Those who are part of God's army but who make idle promises or speak deceitfully to the faithful soldiers in God's army will be unable to make the faithful soldiers weary. Guard against such people.

> [But the Lord rebukes Jeremiah's impatience, saying] If you have raced with men on foot and they have tired you out, then how can you compete with horses? And if [you take to flight] in a land of peace where you feel secure, then what will you do [when you tread the tangled maze of jungle haunted by lions] in the swelling and flooding of the Jordan? For even your brethren and the house of your father—even they have dealt treacherously with you; yes, even they are [like a pack of hounds] in full cry after you. Believe them not, though they speak fair words and promise good things to you.

## God Promises Rest for the Weary

In other examples God's Word teaches us that our Commander will be faithful to provide times of rest and refreshing to His faithful soldiers. Job 3:17 speaks of a place in the spirit where the wicked cease from troubling and the weary will have rest. In Isaiah 28:12 the word of the Lord spoke to God's people concerning a rest that causes the weary to rest and a refreshing from the Lord, *but they would not hear.*

We are taught in our operations guidebook to share in the sufferings and hardships of others, and we have learned that a good soldier is always looking out for the needs of his fellow soldiers. Isaiah 50:4 teaches that we should know how to speak a word in season to the weary.

Our Commander will never overlook the needs of the faithful soldier who is doing the work assigned to him or her. Jeremiah 31:25 teaches us that God will satisfy every weary soul and replenish every sorrowful person. In Jeremiah 51:58 we discover that our Commander will thwart the efforts of our enemies, and that instead of being able to make us weary with their warfare tactics, *they will be made weary by God our Commander.*

Hear the Word of the Lord, saints in America; be not weary in well-doing, but rest and be refreshed! God will reward your faithfulness to the work of the kingdom. Stay focused on your mission and be faithful in your prayers. The efforts of your enemies will not be able to hinder your faithfulness in prayer. The apostles in the Bible were warned by the false religious leaders not to pray in Jesus's name. Daniel was told not to pray at all. In each instance the men of God obeyed Him and remained faithful in their prayer lives, even while under attack and great threat. The power of prayer is unlimited in the midst of persecution. Be the voice that will cry out in the wilderness. Open your window, face Jerusalem, and pray in Jesus's name alone. He is God, and He is with us! May the anointing of Emmanuel be with you as you join us in prayer to get on our faces, on the walls, in the gates, and in the gaps of America! God bless!

God will be faithful to you and will provide you with the times of refreshing and rest you need. God laid out the fortieth chapter of Isaiah to minister comfort to those whom the enemy is trying to wear out. As your expanded study on this important topic of not becoming weary in the work of God, go to Appendix A, "Section

8-1: Do Not Be Weary in Well-Doing: Isaiah 40," and read these encouraging words from your Commander. They will renew your spirit and give you renewed energy to stay faithful to the mission you have received as a soldier in God's army.

# PART THREE

## SPIRITUAL DISCIPLINES

The soldier in God's army must learn to continually grow in his or her abilities to carry out the mission the Commander has given for that soldier to do. Just as the soldier in the United States Army is expected to develop, sustain, and improve his or her competencies for performing assigned tasks, so too the spiritual soldier should continuously refine and extend his or her abilities to perform proficiently, ever learning to apply spiritual disciplines to increasingly complex spiritual situations. This section on spiritual disciplines will give you the tools to be the best you can be for your Commander.

## Chapter 9

# PROTOCOL AND PROCEDURE, PART 1

I RECENTLY RECEIVED A 911 call from an old friend from my past. My friend was heavily involved in the black arts or, to be more specific, in witchcraft. He had lost my number and had contacted one of my family members to alert me that he was in a tight situation. My friend has given his life to the Lord, which is a miracle based on how far he was engrafted into darkness. His situation was so stressful that he was having strong thoughts of resorting to witchcraft to deal with it. I praise God that he contacted me.

He was in an intense controversy with a close family member who is a witch. I consoled my friend and reminded him that we served the Most High God and victory was his. I committed to pray with him over the matter, but for two days after my commitment I could not connect with him on the phone. Things that could not be explained were happening to both of our phone lines to keep us from communicating. I knew that I was in another level of warfare.

You may be asking yourself how this situation relates to a spiritual boot camp. I can answer that question easily. If you are in a warlike situation, you had better know who your enemy is, how he operates, and how to deal with him. In this chapter I am giving you information that is not for the general population of soldiers. This is secret intelligence data that you must have a special clearance to receive.

The military has three levels of clearances:

---

- *General clearance*—all enlisted soldiers have background checks and basic records checks.
- *Secret clearance*—these were clearances given for a smaller group because they were given accessibility to pertinent information that was only given on a need-to-know basis.
- *Top secret clearance*—this is the highest level of clearance in the armed forces. It is only given to a small select group, and the background check is so intense it is unimaginable.

---

The information I am about to discuss is top secret in the body of Christ. This clearance comes from a Holy Ghost investigation of your heart. The requirement is that you be delivered from your past and truly want to know the whole truth and nothing but the truth. The general population of the church is not ready for the whole truth. They only want to know enough truth to protect them and pay their bills. The truth that I am giving in this chapter requires a clearing of your heart to forget what you thought you knew and to be open to what is really going on.

I met an attorney recently as I was operating in my profession as an elected official. We were at an event, and she broke down. She has a personal situation that just hit her hard in the middle of a business meeting. I pulled her off to console her without the other attorneys taking notice. When we talked the next day, I received a true revelation of the carnal mind. I told her that she was the most carnally minded person I had ever met in my life. And based on the number of people I have dealt with, that's huge!

Her situation was so bad. I told her that the devil was attacking her in a big way. The problem was that she did not believe in the devil. As respectfully as I could, I let her know that she would never get out of her situation. She was shocked. I went on further to explain that if she did not acknowledge the source of her problem, the issue could never be settled. She was a churchgoing woman, and she confessed that she believed in God but denied the existence of the devil. I told her that if there was a heaven, there was a hell, and if there was a God, there was a devil. She asked me how I could pair the two, and she said that she only wanted to stick to what was in the Bible. I let her know that she needed to pray and read her Bible again! It is amazing how people pick parts of the Word and literally skim over what they subliminally do not want to know. My advice to anyone who does this is to go back to the parts you skipped over, and you will find that this is exactly what you need.

Thinking back again to my friend who called asking for my help, I know that some people may not be able to fathom that a person who has given his life to Christ would even consider going back to the black arts to handle problems in his life. Please refrain from judging him until I go unto further details about the situation. If you have never been exposed to this level of spiritual warfare, you would not know where to begin in considering the matter. I had to reach deep in my spirit and minister to my friend. There was a battle going on, and his soul was the bounty. I could not judge him. God gave me compassion to relate to the attack he was under. He had been a high-level warlock, and the spirits that he had been delivered from were knocking on the door of his heart (house) to make him seven times worse.

> But when the unclean spirit has gone out of a man, it roams through dry [arid] places in search of rest, but it does not find any. Then it says, I will go back to my house from which I came out. And when it arrives, it finds the place unoccupied, swept, put in order, and decorated. Then it goes and brings with it seven other spirits more wicked than itself, and they go in and make their home there. And the last condition of that

> man becomes worse than the first. So also shall it be with this wicked generation.
>
> —MATTHEW 12:43–45

The devil does not respect the fact that we are new creatures in Christ Jesus. He is reprobate. He held the highest position in heaven and still does not get it. No matter what you have been delivered from, there is one gatekeeper watching you and trying to figure out a way to open the door for his buddies to come in and make you seven times worse.

This is why so many people in the church struggle. They do not understand that the more anointed you are, the greater the assignment of Satan to take what God has done in your life. I stand on the fact that he whom the Son has made free is free indeed. But the truth is, even though the Son has set you free, you must walk out your salvation with fear and trembling. The Bible says that if it were possible, even the very elect would be deceived and the righteous would scarcely make it into the kingdom.

After being enlisted into the United States Armed Forces, it is not necessarily automatic that the soldier will retire from the military or even complete his or her tour of duty. There are several ways that military members do not finish the course that is set before them:

---

- Some are killed by friendly fire.
- Some become a casualty of war.
- Some receive a physical disability discharge.
- Some receive a mental or emotional disability discharge.
- Some receive an administrative discharge.
- Others receive a discharge based upon their job performance incompetence.
- Still others receive a dishonorable discharge.

---

There may be other ways that a military member can be discharged, but these are the ones that come to my mind. The one that I would like to focus on is the *dishonorable discharge*. The last thing that you want is a dishonorable discharge from God's armed forces.

In 1 Corinthians 9:25–28 Paul describes the careful steps he took to ensure that he did not receive a dishonorable discharge from God:

> Now every athlete who goes into training conducts himself temperately and restricts himself in all things. They do it to win a wreath that will soon wither, but we [do it to receive a crown of eternal blessedness] that cannot wither. Therefore I do not run uncertainly (without definite aim). I do not box like one beating the air and striking without an adversary. But [like a boxer] I buffet my body [handle it roughly, discipline it by hardships] and subdue it, for fear that after proclaiming to others the Gospel and things pertaining to it, I myself should become unfit [not stand the test, be unapproved and rejected as a counterfeit].

Paul continued by opening up and confessing his weakness. There is not a human being who does not have a weakness. This is why we need the Holy Spirit in our lives. We all fall short of the glory of God!

Paul was a real man with real challenges in his life. He was a soldier in God's army who knew the secrets of the other side. God gave him a top secret clearance in the kingdom of God. He was honored to write most of the New Testament, but he still understood that the course ahead of him was not automatically conquered. Paul understood the battle plan. He compared his plight to that of an athlete. He made it clear that even the best athletes would not receive the prize without discipline. He also made it clear that he was not speaking of an earthly prize but of a *crown of eternal blessedness*.

Paul identified two enemies against his spiritual discipline:

---

1. His body (which he handled roughly and disciplined by hardships)
2. An unseen but very real adversary (which he could not just swing at air against but needed a strategy against)

---

In 2 Corinthians 12:7–10 Paul told it like it really was:

> And to keep me from being puffed up and too much elated by the exceeding greatness (preeminence) of these revelations, there was given me a thorn (a splinter) in the flesh, a messenger of Satan, to rack and buffet and harass me, to keep me from being excessively exalted. Three times I called upon the Lord and besought [Him] about this and begged that it might depart from me; but He said to me, My grace (My favor and loving-kindness and mercy) is enough for you [sufficient against any danger and enables you to bear the trouble manfully]; for My strength and power are made perfect (fulfilled and completed) and show themselves most effective in [your] weakness.
>
> Therefore, I will all the more gladly glory in my weaknesses and infirmities, that the strength and power of Christ (the Messiah) may rest (yes, may pitch a tent over and dwell) upon me! So for the sake of Christ, I am well pleased and take pleasure in infirmities, insults, hardships, persecutions, perplexities and distresses; for when I am weak [in human strength], then am I [truly] strong (able, powerful in divine strength).

Paul described his strategy for being victorious over the devil who was trying to hinder him from his course. He listed the following steps:

- Paul confessed that he had a serious issue in his life from which he was not delivered.
- He believed that God allowed it to be so that he would not get puffed up or excessively exalted.
- Paul asked God to deliver him three times, to no avail.
- God's response to Paul was that His grace was sufficient.
- Paul accepted the will of God and took pleasure in his hardships.
- He concluded that when he was weak, God's divine strength was perfected in him.

When I talked with my friend who was considering going back to witchcraft, although I could not relate to being there, I understood where my friend was. A big problem is that there are so many lukewarm churches that have members who do not study the full gospel. Because they are ignorant of the wiles and devices of the enemy, they cannot discern between what is holy and what is common.

There are many religious spirits in the church that actually dibble and dabble in the occult in Jesus's name and believe that they are licensed to do so. They operate in white magic, horoscopes, fetishism, superstition, necromancy, and entertain psychic spirits but still attend church every Sunday. I am not condemning people for participating in these things if this is what they believe in. I am saying that these are not biblical practices for believers and are forbidden by God in His Word. People who operate in this realm paint the wrong picture and have no positive witness to those who come to Jesus from the occult world.

People from the other side ask me, "Why should I give up the deep things of darkness when church folk dibble and dabble? Is a small sin better than a big one?" The answer to this question is an easy one. *All sin will be judged—small or big, knowingly or unknowingly, white magic, black magic, or charismatic* (*church*) *magic*. From the pulpit to the heathen on the streets, every human being will be accountable to God in the end. Our guide in the end is the unadulterated Word of Jesus Christ.

## Chapter 10

# PROTOCOL AND PROCEDURE, PART 2

When it comes to military affairs, getting the job done by any means necessary is the vision. Because the armed forces have so many departments, leaders, ranks, and realms of authority, consistency is a must. The general protocol and procedures for military affairs in Germany are the same in the United States. This principle holds the same in God's army. Ephesians 4:5 says that there is one Lord, one faith, and one baptism. In Philippians 1:27 Paul reminds us that we must stand fast in one spirit, with one mind for the faith of the gospel (one gospel).

As we walk in the gifts of God and stand in faith, the scriptures above, along with 1 Corinthians 12:4–6, outline proper protocol.

> Now there are distinctive varieties and distributions of endowments (gifts, extraordinary powers distinguishing certain Christians, due to the power of divine grace operating in their souls by the Holy Spirit) and they vary, but the [Holy] *Spirit remains the same.* And there are distinctive varieties of service and ministration, but it is *the same Lord* [Who is served]. And there are distinctive varieties of operation [of working to accomplish things], but it is *the same God* Who inspires and energizes them all in all.
>
> —Emphasis added

Even when it comes to spiritual things, God has a protocol and procedures. It is important to understand the definition for both.

---

1. *Protocol*—formal etiquette and code of behavior, precedence, or procedure on how this should be carried out
2. *Procedure*—A particular course or mode of action

---

Many people just attend church but never study to show themselves approved concerning the things of God. This is very dangerous and can lead to having a form of godliness and denial of the true power of God. As a result our churches are infiltrated with people who look like Christians, go to church faithfully, and know all the antics of being a church person, but in reality they operate by another spirit with counterfeit power. They do not come as three-dollar bills because they can be easily recognized as counterfeit. Instead they present themselves as ten-, fifty-, and one-hundred-dollar bills. They look just like the real things.

Those who oppose what I am teaching would argue that everyone should be able to attend our churches. I agree from a conditional standpoint. They can come as long as they understand and get with the program. Faith is a powerful thing, and people of like faith should worship together. I agree that everyone has the right to worship, but a part of that right is that they have a right to contend for their faith. After all, this is what America is all about. The Jews have a right to celebrate the Sabbath, the Muslims have a right to pray to the east, and Christians should have a right to have places of worship to obey the Word of the Lord—*one Lord, one faith, one baptism*!

Anyone who wants to come into my AO (area of operation) has to get an understanding that we operate by the standard that the Lord has raised, and lowering that standard is not an option. Using any power outside of the power of God is not an option for me. My power ends where God's begins, because without Him I am nothing.

After the blessing has come and the miracle has taken place, I have to have clean hands. Many have blood on their hands for manipulating the spirit realm in and of their own flesh. Jesus rose from the dead and declared, "I have all power in My hands!" I believe what He said. For those who choose to resort to taking shortcuts in the spirit realm, they may be subject to getting off the road to the promise and never getting back on again.

To violate the protocol and procedures of God is a serious thing. Just getting blessed is enough—the important key is with *how you get a so-called blessing.* I want blessings that keep my hands clean at the end of the day. I want more than results; I want the will of God. There are ways that seem right in the eyes of man, but they are dead ends (and lead to death). You can gain the entire world and lose your soul in the end.

It is true...the effectual, fervent prayers of the righteous avail much, but in the availing we must come out with clean hands. Dirty hands come from dirty hearts. Witchcraft flows fluently through dirty hearts. James said it best:

> Draw near to God and He will draw near to you. Cleanse your hands, you sinners; and purify your hearts, you double-minded.
>
> —James 4:8, nkjv

James addressed two kinds of people in this passage of Scripture: sinners, and the double-minded.

Who are the double-minded? I believe this term refers to people who cannot make up their minds on whom they want to serve. This has been a spiritual struggle throughout the history of the Bible.

- Joshua made the statement that along with his house, he would serve the Lord (Josh. 24:15). Apparently there was some double-mindedness in the camp.

- Moses said that whoever was on the Lord's side needed to stand with him. The ground opened up and swallowed those who did not join Moses (Num. 16:24–31). This crew of double-minded people had second thoughts about who God had put in charge.

- Elijah stood on Mount Carmel and said that people should either serve God or the devil. The community was divided and had not made a strong commitment to either Baal or the god of Abraham, Isaac, and Jacob (1 Kings 18:21).

When it comes to the promises of God and obeying Him, we cannot be double-minded. When trouble comes, being double-minded is not an option. In times like this a strange voice will come to try to make you second-guess the power of God and who you are in Him. In the good times and in the bad times remember that *a double-minded man gets no results from God.*

Many people manipulate the spirit realm (in Jesus's name) and get results. The problem with this is that in doing so, they violate spiritual integrity. Spiritual integrity causes a person to understand what I call the *mystery of power.* Understanding the mystery of power is simply having the revelation that God has all power, but the devil operates in a counterfeit power. This power is a reality to the ones (on the other side) who believe in it and a danger to those who ignore it. The mystery of power presents the fact that there is power on both sides. God has power, and the devil has a counterfeit power.

I will say it again—how you get blessed and the source of your breakthrough matters. The truth is... *the devil can bless you!*

Abraham, the father of faith, had to get this revelation. The king of Sodom tried to bless Abraham, but the father of the faith came to the conclusion that he could not let the devil bless him. Abraham's blessing was bigger than him. His blessing then is a part of my blessing today; I serve the God of Abraham, Isaac, and Jacob. Abraham understood that he was at the brink of receiving a generational blessing or a generational curse. Instead of taking that one-time blessing from the king of Sodom (which represented the devil), he allowed God to bless him through the order of Melchizedek (which represented and was a foreshadow of Christ). He told the king of Sodom, "I cannot allow you to bless me because you will get the credit (glory)!" (See Genesis 14.)

This is a very important principle to remember and pass on throughout your generations. Whoever or whatever is the source of your blessing, that person or thing will get the credit (glory) in the end. God wants to bless us, and He wants the honor, the glory, and the praise for it. God wants the credit for the accomplishments in our lives. We know that He will use people, places, and things to open doors that no man can deny, but when the rubber hits the road, God must be honored as the root source.

It is also important to note that when the devil blesses you, there is an unseen interest levy placed on it. This reminds me of my military days before I got saved and started paying my tithes. I was addicted to going to the pawn shop outside the post gate to get advances on my pay every month. The problem was that it was a bottomless hole that I could never get out of. I had to give a copy of my Leave and Earning Statement (LES), and they automatically deducted the amount borrowed, *with interest*! I was robbing Peter to pay Paul. I did not get out of this trap until I got my life right with God and started paying my tithes and offerings. Before that I was financially living paycheck to paycheck, month to month, day to day.

I can easily compare this to going to psychics, reading dream books, getting words from false prophets for money, and outright operating in the dark arts through fetishism, numerology, and getting readings from people whose roots are connected with a source outside of God. The crazy thing about all of this is that it really works. The reality of it all is that there is an ungodly interest attached that will be a great price to pay.

There are people who ignorantly operate in this realm of deception. On the other hand there are people who have full understanding of what they are doing but do not have enough discipline to wait on God, or they simply just want something that works.

I am proud to testify that the things of God work. People just need to get in place to work them. As people of God we cannot shout *abracadabra*, say *open sesame*, and wave a magic wand and get a breakthrough for a blessing. Standing on the truth is the key. The part of standing that people do not like the most is *waiting on God*:

> But they that wait upon the Lord shall renew their strength; they shall mount up with wings as eagles; they shall run and not be weary; and they shall walk, and *not faint*.
>
> —Isaiah 40:31, KJV, emphasis added

> And thou shalt know that I am the Lord: for they shall *not be ashamed* that wait for me.
>
> —Isaiah 49:23, KJV, emphasis added

## The Rewards of Waiting on the Lord

In the last chapter I told you about my friend who came to me because he was being tempted to return to witchcraft to get an answer to an urgent need. He was minutes away from going to the root man for a quick fix. Instead we prayed; I spoke the Word of God into his spirit, and the scales were removed from his eyes. These two passages above are the insurance (or assurance) policies for his situation—and those you may be facing. Though he was getting opposition from high-level witchcraft in a familiar position, waiting on the Lord was his answer. No matter how bad things get, we must have the confidence that if God is for us, no one can be against us. It is true that if we wait on God we will be lifted above our circumstances, and we will not be ashamed (damned).

I just prayed with my friend about five hours ago. We prayed for his mother who was having physical attacks every day at noon. I stopped writing this chapter to call my friend. The report of the Lord is that for the first time in a while, his mother did not get attacked at noon. These attacks lasted for exactly two hours (until 2:00 P.M.). This was evidence to me that this was a time-released curse. We did territorial warfare and took authority over this lie.

The truth is that Jesus has all power and the devil is a fraud. He was trespassing because a door was opened. This is called a *squatting spirit*. We kicked the devil out and closed the door. It was not a coincidence that the attacks were coming at noon. There is a curse called the *high noon curse*. It reminds me of the old western days. In the wild, wild west it was usual for people to be called into the middle of the streets for showdowns at high noon.

Even today the enemy likes to call believers out on front-street in the spirit to challenge the Lordship of their Savior, Jesus Christ. He has a heyday with unarmed believers who do not know their authority in God. On the other hand, when the devil calls out an armed believer, it is his worst nightmare. The gallows that he built for that believer hangs his stuff out to dry in front of everyone. When this happens, we get delivered and God gets what He wants...THE GLORY!

My friend and I met the devil at noon, and we were strapped. We were quickened by the Holy Spirit to disarm the enemy and kick him out of the house. Is Jesus the sheriff of your home?

## Dealing With the Occult

There is a principle that is understood by witches who take the time to study their craft. All witches are dumb (what really smart person would come against the Most High God?), but most of them are unlearned. They use roots, dolls, and fetishes (objects with demons attached) and practice all sorts of darkness from a blind side. They do not take the time to consider what they are really dealing with. They just want results, never considering the repercussions. I do not believe that there are a large percentage of people who willingly serve the devil and work on his side. The enemy blindsides many to ignorantly worship him through familiar spirits, cultures, religion, or the quest for wealth and power.

Another side of the story is that there is a small community of people who worship the devil and literally believe that he is Lord. Just as we look forward to going to heaven, they believe that they will reign with Lucifer (the fallen angel) in hell.

There are many categories of people who willingly operate on the dark side. I reminded my friend of my encounter with some of them when the devil was attacking his mind. The following story is one example.

Years ago I received a call from a distressed mother who claimed her daughter was a teenage witch. I called one of my ministers, and we connected to the mom and her daughter on a three-way phone call. The young lady started the conversation by bragging about how preachers were afraid of her. She told me how she put hooks in her body and hung from the ceiling. She said that she conjured spirits and had constant communication with the dead. She also told me how she had already astral projected to my house before we spoke and described things in my house. She told me that she was a white Wiccan witch and that she did not operate in the dark arts, but she took pride in having more power than weak Christian preachers.

Immediately I realized that I was dealing with a proud, evil spirit in the young girl, so I dealt with the spirit. I refused to allow the spirit in her to make me fear. God has not given me a spirit of fear but of power, love, and a sound mind. This was what I stood on:

- The spirit of boldness to confront every rebellious spirit that stood against the truth
- The fact that the greater One was in me and not in her
- The love of God that gave me compassion for her soul in spite of her insubordination to the King of kings
- A balance in my mind concerning the wisdom for how to confront this spirit and leave open a door for the salvation of her soul.
- Taking a mental posture that there were no *ifs*, *ands*, or *buts* about who I was in Jesus

I did not pray for the young lady during our encounter. She was just simply not ready. Her mother was a Christian, and I could feel her pain through the phone. Her daughter was a sixteen-year-old who dressed in black, was obsessed with piercing and tattooing her body, and admitted to being a witch that hated God.

I told the young lady that she and I needed to make a deal. I told her to send every curse she could to my house over the next seven days (since she had been there in the spirit). I told her that I would pray to my God and she could do her thing, and we would meet on the phone again in seven days. I told her to send sickness, failure, death, and anything else she could conjure up against me. I asked her if she would agree that if I was all right when we spoke again, that she would change her allegiance to my God.

Her answer shocked me. She said, "I can't." She explained that her craft taught her that if she ever sent a curse against God's anointed, whatever she sent would come back on her three times. Later many others trying to come out of the occult to the Lord's side told me the same thing. It is called the *threefold curse*. For some reason witches who have studied their craft believe this.

I do know that it is biblical to reap what you have sown, and if you sow to the flesh, you will reap of it. Witchcraft is a work of the flesh. Also, in the Book of Ecclesiastes, the Bible speaks about a threefold cord not being easily broken. Could it be that when witches come against the children of the Trinity (the Father, Son, and the Holy Ghost), the repercussions relate to what they have come against?

In closing this chapter, I want to remind all—recruits, trainees, soldiers, and leaders—that in God's army protocol and procedure are everything. But there can be no protocol without honoring authority, the respect for order, and having a revelation of submission to the chain of command. If you are reading this book and are usurping authority or thinking more of yourself when it comes to these things, hear the word of the Lord...*Stand down, soldier!* If you do not know what I mean, I will expound in the next chapter.

## Chapter 11

# A GOOD SOLDIER KNOWS HOW TO STAND DOWN

THE WORDS *STAND down* have been ringing in my spirit for the past few weeks. I have had the opportunity to staff a high-level elected official recently, and it has been a learning experience. I have always said that it is a good balance for leaders to serve others who have a higher position over them. Well, this was my opportunity. I have always served my apostle, John Eckhardt, when I am with him. I have to lay down my own status as author, international speaker, and elected official to serve him when I am with him. I have to keep my eyes on my apostle and make sure that he is taken care of.

To staff an official in my profession is the same as being an armor bearer in the church. You are required to make sure the person being staffed is prepared to do whatever they are assigned to do. These duties may include making reservations, driving, packing suitcases for travel, getting meals, or just simply troubleshooting when situations arise. In essence you become the *go-to* person on the mission. I thank God for this opportunity, because it gave me a chance to see things from another perspective. The pressure is intense, but at the end of the day it is fulfilling to know that you made things happen. It feels good to know that a person of such a high-level position can depend on you to get the job done. People who hold positions like this have a lot of responsibility, and their minds need to be clear of all of the minute things that have to be done. Though these things are minute in nature, they need to be effectively carried out so that the overall mission will not be hindered. Something as simple a mistake as not providing a car when it is needed can deter a major assignment.

Out of the experience I learned one thing. I need to train the people who directly assist me to go to another level. We must be shakers and movers, and *dropping the ball* is unacceptable. We can do better. Spirits of rejection, insecurity, shame, pride, low self-esteem, man-pleasing, and simply not knowing who you are will make you hide shortcomings instead of exposing them so that they can be dealt with.

## Important Terms

There are some important military terms that also carry great spiritual significance for the soldier in God's army. These terms have always helped me in serving and with developing leadership skills. They include:

---

1. *Dropping the ball.* This is a very important term. If an assignment is given, it must be carried out. There are no excuses for things not getting done. It is obvious that obstacles will occur in any mission, but the key is, *never drop the ball!* Even if you cannot make a task happen, find a person who can. If the assignment is absolutely impossible, do not leave loose ends. Go to the person who gave the assignment and let them know about the obstacle and discuss it from there. NEVER let the assignment be put on the back burner without discussing the matter with your superior. It is a terrible thing to be uninformed about an assignment you have given when it is in limbo. The person assigning the task may have input that may be able to solve the problem. The spirit to be aware of is *pride*. Never allow pride to make you hide the details of a problem. The Bible says that two are better than one, and you cannot lose when you put your thoughts with the thoughts of your superior.

2. *Delegation of authority.* This is the ability of a leader to recognize professionals under his or her authority who can manage people, places, or things in excellence and with proficiency without their intervention.
3. *Micromanagement.* This happens when a leader does not have the ability to release assignments to others. The leader is obsessed with having his or her hands on all levels of the mission. This will eventually lead to burnout if not addressed.
4. *Chain of command.* This is the order set in place to designate the levels of authority and to whom each person involved reports.
5. *Usurping of authority.* This happens when an individual takes on assignments above his or her pay grade, tries to get ahead of the set order by doing things that are not authorized, overrides the limitations of the job description or duty assignment, and promotes himself or herself, consciously or unconsciously.
6. *Obeying a lawful order.* Submission to constituted authority and respect and adherence to orders is given without veering off from them.
7. *Staying in formation.* This involves maintaining the synchronization of the order set, usually when gatherings are set for accountability and information. It also enables orderly movement such as in aircraft formation or the movement of marching troops.
8. *Standing down.* This order is given to cease all action; it's a suspension from a state of alertness or readiness to a state of rest, a military command that orders a temporary stop of an offensive move or action.

---

## Standing Down

I have touched on most of these terms in my previous books. Recently God has given me a revelation of the last term listed: *standing down*. I believe that what I have learned about this term is one of the more important principles on leadership in the kingdom that I have ever learned. First I would like to say that I have always understood respecting the position even if the person did not deserve respect. Promotion does not come for the east, west, or south; it comes from the north, which is the secret place of God. So if God is the One ultimately behind promotion, there is an anointing in positions that must be respected.

Now let me give the balance. I would never follow a person off a cliff or yield my spirit to anything antichrist, but on the other hand I am required by the Word of God to respect those in governmental leadership, ministerial leadership, and elders in age.

While working as an elected official, someone who outranked me gave me an assignment. The person who was doing the assignment before me had a problem with the way I was carrying out things. The higher-ranking official ordered that person to *stand down*. The official explained that this was not that person's assignment anymore, and the way things were carried out should no longer be that person's concern. Those words, *stand down*, continued to ring in my mind, and I thought, "There are so many people in the church who need to stand down."

Recently I finally saw the movie about the Tuskegee airmen. The movie was very inspirational, but I got a better revelation of the term *stand down* while watching it. There was a headstrong pilot in the movie who was the best at what he did. He took chances on every mission. He was gung-ho about being a black pilot taking out Nazi fighter pilots. His name was Lightning, and every victory gave him more pride and power.

Lightning had a commanding pilot over him whom he always disobeyed. He had several victories that he got despite disobeying the lawful orders of his commanding supervisor. This went well for a while. Eventually his disrespect for orders from his chain of command caught up with him. On his last mission he made a big move and took out an entire Nazi aircraft carrier. He would always go in close to the enemy and come out with a big victory. He took out the carrier, but as he was bragging over the radio to his commanding officer, he spit up blood. He had been fatally wounded and did not even know it. He got the victory but died earlier than he had to.

He was possessed with the zeal for his next level of victory. Sometimes wisdom and experience can override skill and zeal. This was the case in Lightning's demise. If he would have followed the orders of his superior, slowed down, and let his gift be seasoned, he would have lived longer.

Spiritually speaking I have witnessed many people in ministry who have become casualties of war. They were young in the things of warfare. They had a zeal but not according to knowledge. The greatest problem was that they felt like they knew more than their teacher. This comes from a familiar spirit. It is easy to become familiar with leaders to the point where you begin to disrespect the position they were given over you.

When I met Apostle John Eckhardt, I had spiritual milk around my mouth. Fourteen years later I have the same publisher that he has, speak at the same conferences, and am a well-sought-after international speaker, just as he is. What draws the line? He is still the teacher, and I am the student. My authority will never override his. He is my pastor; I am not his!

Selling a trillion books or getting a million members will never change this. The order has been set. When I escort him places and people come to me for autographs and so forth, I let them know that I cannot sign books then because I am serving my apostle. I feel the same way when I am staffing the elected official God has honored me to serve. Even with my approximately ninety-three thousand votes, I am still the student. This official has been where I am trying to go. How could I dare to walk by that person's side and compare my eight months in office to that person's tenure, which has endured over three decades?

Though we are called to be bold and be all that we can be in the armed forces of the Lord, the greatest wisdom and the seeds for endurance is to have the discernment of how and when to *stand down*.

A terrible thing has taken place in the state of Florida that is shaking our nation. A seventeen-year-old boy was gunned down in a gated community. He was profiled as a criminal, when the young boy had only a pack of Skittles candy and a can of iced tea in his possession. The 911 recording showed that the man who gunned the boy down called in to say a suspicious person was walking through the community. The police dispatcher ordered the man to *stand down*. They ordered him to cease following the young man. In the end a young man has died uselessly. The gunman was a neighborhood watch captain who apparently took his job too seriously. He had just enrolled in criminology courses. He had a concealed weapons license, but he operated above his pay grade and usurped an authority that he did not have.[1]

My prayer is that whatever your assigned capacity in the boot camp of the Lord, you will know your assignment, respect the authority placed over you, and have the discernment in knowing the difference in the time to *stand up* or *stand down*.

## Chapter 12

# BOOT CAMP FINANCIAL PRINCIPLES

HOW COULD ANYONE be a soldier for the Lord without adherence to the financial principles of God? The first thing that the Lord revealed to me as a new believer was about the principle of tithing. It is a basic training discipline. We cannot be disciples of the Lord without applying this discipline to our lives. The tenth belongs to the Lord. Let's take a look at Old and New Testament scriptures that tell us why we pay our tithes.

### WHY DO WE PAY OUR TITHES?

The Bible says that the tithe is holy unto the Lord: "And all the tithe of the land, whether of the seed of the land or of the fruit of the tree, is the Lord's; it is holy to the Lord" (Lev. 27:30). Let us take a look at the word *holy*. The Hebrew word for "holy," *qodesh*, means, "dedicated thing." When something is dedicated, it is set apart and consecrated for special use.

Dedications are related to covenants in the way that they are *foundational agreements*. Dedications lay foundations for a thing in the spirit. The "accursed thing" (Josh. 6:18) lays a foundation for (or gives root to) for the things of the devil, but that which is dedicated unto holiness lays a foundation for (or gives root to) the things of God. When something is dedicated, it is *given* for a particular purpose. In the natural we have baby dedications, house and property dedications, and church dedications. During dedications we present these things unto the Lord as separated unto Him for His use. So it is with the tithe. The tithe is holy, dedicated, or separated unto the Lord. This part of our income must be separated from our hearts. When we give our tithes, we must release ourselves from them in our minds. It is a sin to pay tithes and worry about what is being done with *your* tithe. In this case true dedication has not taken place. We cannot follow the tithe from the altar to the bank and say that separation has taken place. We must pray as to where God wants us to fellowship and fully release our tithe by faith. Tithing without faith does not please God. A dirty heart or wrong spirit makes the true purpose of tithing null and void.

Ever since Cain and Abel God made it clear that we could not give Him what *we wanted* to give Him. Though tithing is for the welfare of the priest and the keeping of God's storehouse, it is unto the Lord. Genesis 4:4 says that Abel gave God the "firstborn" of his flock, and the Lord had respect for it. He brought the chief or best part. He presented God with his best. Though in this day we do not offer God goats and calves (in Bible times animals were given as a type of currency), God still wants the best of our increase.

The importance of this topic is not money or goats; it is about "seedtime and harvest." Genesis 8:22 tells us that as long as the earth remains, there will be seedtime and harvest. This word *seedtime* is *zera* in the Hebrew, and it is defined as sowing time. We can safely say that as long as the earth remains, the spiritual principles of God will be set in place.

The first place that the word *tithe* is mentioned in the Bible is in the Book of Leviticus. In this book tithes are described as holy or separated unto the Lord. I believe that the first thing God wants us to know is that the principle of tithing is holy or separated unto Him. Once we understand the principle, the act will become a part of life. God is so merciful that He allowed us to be stewards of all that is His. The entire earth is the Lord's and the fullness thereof. Yes, Psalm 24:1 says that not only does the whole earth belong to the Lord, but He also owns everything that is in it. God is so wonderful that He gave Adam dominion over all the earth (Gen. 1:26). The devil came in and infiltrated the plan. All of a sudden man had an enemy to contend with concerning his inheritance or place in God.

Throughout the Old Testament God gave man instructions on tithing:

---

- Jacob promised the tithe to God (Gen. 28:22).
- The tithe was holy to the Lord and was not to be redeemed by man (Lev. 27:30–33).
- The tithe was given to the Levites for an inheritance in return for their service in the tabernacle (Num. 18:21–24).
- The Levites were to present a tithe of what was given to them to Aaron, the high priest, who would present it to the Lord (Num. 18:25–28).
- When the Israelites settled in the Promised Land, they were instructed to take the tithe of their wine and oil, their grain and crops, and of their herds and flocks as an offering to the Lord and give it to the Levites at the temple (Deut. 12:17–19).
- The Lord established specific instructions regarding the tithe (Deut. 14:22–29).
- When Nehemiah discovered that the tithe had been neglected in Jerusalem during the time that some of the Jews were in bondage in Babylon, forcing the Levites to leave their duties in the temple to work in the fields, he cleansed the temple, reinstituted the tithe, and set treasurers in place to guard the distribution of the tithe correctly (Neh. 13:5–13).

---

The truth of the matter was (and still is) that an offering could not be made until the tithe was initiated first. What I mean is that you cannot give a person above what you already owe them. One of the Hebrew definitions for the word *tithe* (*apodekatoō*) is to pay as a debt. So we *pay* our tithes and *give* offerings. It would be absurd if I *owed* you $550 to tell you that I was *giving* you $350. I would not be *giving* you anything; I would still owe you $200! We cannot give anything as an offering unto the Lord until we have first met the requirements of what He has declared that we owe Him. It is not as though God needs anything from us except our obedience. It is our obedience that He wants. It is better than sacrifice. Another Hebrew word for "tithe" is *asar,* which means:

---

- To accumulate
- To grow
- To make rich
- The way to wealth

---

## God's Principle for Gaining Wealth

Tithing is the biblical principle that God laid out for His people to grow and get wealth. Wealth does not just include financial and material increase; it also includes the peace, health, welfare, and protection of the people of God. God wants us to know that it is He who has given us the power to get wealth (Deut. 8:18). He gave us this power to establish His covenant with us.

Tithing is a covenant principle. Our Father allows us to have stewardship over all that is His and only requires that 10 percent be given back to Him. We can spend 90 percent (of what really belongs to God) at our own discretion. This is a tight covenant! God promises that if we obey Him by putting Him first in our increase, He will make us prosper. Tithing gives us the power to get wealth. God wants our first love. He can measure if we are really giving our first love when we give Him our firstfruits.

> For where your treasure is, there will your heart be also.
>
> —Matthew 6:21

Proverbs 3:9 tells us that when we give God our substance and the firstfruits of our increase, we honor Him. If this is the case, we dishonor the Lord when we do not give Him our best. What is the best? The best is to give God what He wants. He wants our obedience. The Hebrew word for "firstfruits" is *re'shiyth* and means, "first in place, time or order." This word also means, "chief" or "principle." God wants to be the first priority is every area of our lives, especially in our finances, because the love of money is the root of all evil (1 Tim. 6:10).

God wants us to avoid the curse of *Gad* and *Meni*. These are the Babylonian gods of fortune and destiny. They are known by the occult world as the *sun god* and *moon goddess*. We have studied them as Nimrod and Semarimis—the queen of heaven and her son. God told Jeremiah not to pray anymore for those who worshipped these gods. The people baked cakes to the queen of heaven for prosperity, and it worked. They boasted that when they baked cakes to the queen of heaven, they prospered. They told God that they would not stop their sacrifices to her because of the benefits (Jer. 44:16–21). Their increase was an ungodly increase!

What does it profit a man to gain the whole world and lose his soul? Many would dare to tempt God with boastfulness in prosperity outside of His principles. There is prosperity outside of the principles or the will of God, but it is called *false prosperity* or *pseudo increase*. In other words, the devil will bless you! It is the kind of increase that does not last long and leads to death. The devil can prosper a person, but it is the grace of God that lets a person fall when he is out of the will of God. My prayer is that if I miss God, please let me fall quickly! Lord, do not allow me to stand in (false) prosperity in the eyes of the people when before You I am wallowing in my vomit.

I would like to answer the question at hand: Why do we pay our tithes? But first I would like to give my stance. I pay tithes because I am a believer and I fear God. Malachi puts it plain as day and night. If we pay our tithes, we are blessed; if we neglect to pay our tithes, we are cursed. Let me emphasize the fact that this is not a regular curse. This curse is implemented with a curse. This word *curse* means to execrate or to dedicate to a curse. It means to loathe and renounce. God says that if we do not dedicate what He wants from us, He will literally turn us over (or dedicate us unto destruction). What does it mean for God to renounce you? If you are reading this study and contemplating the idea of not paying your tithes, let me discourage you from this act. Malachi stated:

> For I am the Lord, I do not change; that is why you, O sons of Jacob, are not consumed. Even from the days of your fathers you have turned aside from My ordinances and have not kept them. Return to me, and I will return to you, says the Lord of hosts. But you say, How shall we return? Will a man rob or defraud God? Yet you rob and defraud Me. But you say, In what way do we rob or defraud You? [You have withheld your] tithes and offerings. You are cursed with the curse, for you are robbing Me, even this whole nation. Bring all the tithes (the whole tenth of your income) into the storehouse, that there may be food in My house, and prove Me now by it, says the Lord of hosts, if I will not open the windows of heaven for you and pour you out a blessing, that there shall not be room enough to receive it. And I will rebuke the devourer [insects and plagues] for your sakes and he shall not destroy the fruits of your ground, neither shall your vine drop its fruit before the time in the field, says the Lord of hosts.
>
> —Malachi 3:6–11

*Whew!* This is enough to put the fear of God in anybody who loves Jesus. Do you know Him as Lord of Creation? If you do, as I do, you won't mess with God's money! God started out by declaring who He was. He said that He does not change. Then He started talking about the tithe. Could He have been talking about the fact that He will never change His mind concerning this issue? God was addressing a people who had left Him. He was commanding them to return to Him. They had left God and did not know how to get back to Him. Why? Because they did not realize how they had left Him. They did not realize that when they kept what they thought was theirs, they robbed God. They asked God, "How will we return to you?" God said, "Pay your tithe and offering!" When we do not pay our tithes, we leave God.

This is so serious! Most preachers have been preaching on paying tithes as if it were an option. They say, "Pay your tithes if you want to be blessed!" This is a life-and-death issue for the born-again believer. We must pay our tithes if we want to live. The hand of the devourer is rebuked for us. The devourer is the one that comes to steal, kill, and destroy.

I believe that God gives us a grace period to come into the revelation of paying our tithes when we get saved. James 4:17 says that any person who knows what is right to do but does not do it, to him it is a sin. On the other hand, continual ignorance in this area will lead to destruction. God says that His people perish for a lack of knowledge.

As we read Malachi the third chapter, several warnings came to my heart:

---

1. If we do not pay our tithes, we are cursed with a curse.
2. If we do not pay our tithes, we affect the increase of God's house and become a hindrance to the kingdom.
3. If we do not pay our tithes, we do not allow God to prove Himself in our lives.
4. If we do not pay our tithes, we live under a closed heaven.

5. If we do not pay our tithes, the devourer has the right to destroy the fruit of our ground.
6. If we do not pay our tithes, we open our lives to spiritual miscarriage.

---

## So Why Do We Pay Our Tithes?

On the streets there are certain people you just do not rob. These people are not robbed because of the power that they have. There are certain gang members or mafia members whose retaliation will be greater than it was worth to rob them. There would be great retaliation if you robbed the wrong drug dealer and someone found out about it. Can you imagine the retaliation of the Lord? Who can hide from Him? The CIA, FBI, and all the federal agencies in the country do not have a system that can track you down like the Holy Ghost. Can you imagine being on a wanted poster (in the Spirit) that God put out on you? I cannot think of better reasons to pay our tithes than these:

---

- We pay our tithes in obedience.
- We pay our tithes out of the fear of God.
- We pay our tithes because we do not want doors to be opened to the devil.
- We pay our tithes because we are not thieves, and only a fool would rob God.

---

God is not jacking us when we do not pay our tithe; we jack ourselves! Tithing is a spiritual principle that was put in place by God Himself. It can work for you or against you. Tithing can be the best thing that ever happened to you, or it can be your worst nightmare. What does this depend on? The principle of tithing will be a friend or foe to you based on where you are in the Spirit. If you are a robber of God, it will be your worst enemy; if you are a faithful in tithing (from your heart), it will be your best friend. Selah!

## Tithing and the New Covenant

When I first came to know Jesus as my Lord and Savior, God revealed the principle of tithing to me before I had a church home. I was saved overseas, and nobody was there to tell me to pay my tithes. I was so new in God I did not know how to pray to dedicate my tithes unto the Lord. I purchased a book called *Prayers That Avail Much.*[1] From that day to this one it has been a joy giving to God what He wants.

We must understand that making God happy is what it is all about. Most people who question tithing today have things in their lives that literally need to be cast out. If you look at it from this perspective, you can never beat God's giving. For the first time in my ministry I recently had a group of people in my church who challenged the principle of tithing. When I was approached, it was unbelievable to me that Spirit-filled people would not believe in tithing. They were precious people whom I could not complain about if I wanted to, but the bottom line is that a spirit deceived them. I must be honest to say that this incident prompted the writing of this study. I repent; I took it for granted that if the Bible says give God 10 percent, then *everyone who claimed to be a believer would adhere to it.*

You must understand that I am hard-hitting with this issue. If you claim to be a believer, have been told about tithing, and refuse to obey in this area, then I question your status as a believer. If the people in Malachi left God when they did not pay their tithes, I do not believe that you will stay with Him if you do the same. Tithing puts us in place in the Spirit. When we neglect tithing, we are out of place in the Spirit.

## Tithing in the New Testament

Let us see what the New Testament says about tithing.

A few people believe that tithing is not for today because it was of the Law. I guess to get a clear understanding of this issue we must review the Law and the transition from the Old Testament to the New Testament. First I must say that the new covenant did not wipe out the old covenant. The new covenant was the fulfillment of what was written in the old covenant.

In Jeremiah 31:33 God said that He would establish another covenant with His people. He said that He would put His law in their inward parts and write it in their hearts. The Law was a schoolmaster that taught us until the coming of the Messiah fulfilled it. God's law was His Word to us. He is the same today, yesterday, and forever more. Heaven and earth will pass away before one dot or tittle of His Word does.

> For truly I tell you, until the sky and earth pass away and perish, not one smallest letter nor one little hook [identifying certain Hebrew letters] will pass from the Law until all things [it foreshadows] are accomplished.
>
> —Matthew 5:18

Though the coming of Jesus is a fulfillment of the Law, all has not been fulfilled. And if all has not been fulfilled, one word from His law shall not pass. It is not God's Word that changed as we went into our new covenant with Him; it is how He applied His law in our lives. The law in our lives is not stone tablets with a list of a bunch of dos and don'ts. Though we still cannot covet or commit adultery or murder, these laws should be written in our hearts. Though our economy does not allow us to give ten goats from one hundred, we can still give God 10 percent of our financial increase. We are in a covenant that takes faith to please God.

Habakkuk said it just right: "The just shall live by his faith" (Hab. 2:4, NKJV). Then Paul took the baton and said that "the righteousness of God is revealed from faith to faith…'The just shall live by faith'" (Rom. 1:17). Righteousness was accounted unto Abraham on credit (because the Messiah had not come), but we do not have to charge what has already been paid for. Jesus paid the ultimate price. It has been from one faith to faith (from the faith that the saints lived by in the Old Testament to the faith that we live by today).

Although there was a transition in the Spirit, has faith changed? I believe it was the same faith that was prophesied in the Old Testament that is manifested in the New. The same faith that was prophesied in Joel 2:28, saying that in the last days God would pour out His Spirit on all flesh, is the same faith revealed and fulfilled in Acts 2:17. If we look at tithing from a natural perspective, we may not believe that it is for today. But the Bible says that the carnal mind will not be able to discern the things of the spirit.

Looking at tithing from a spiritual perspective, it was before and after the Law. Tithing was a part of the Law but not limited there. The Bible tells us that Abraham paid a tenth of his increase to Melchizedek. You must have a spiritual eye to discern who Melchizedek was. The Bible says that He has no beginning and no ending. Let us look at what the Bible says.

Hebrew 7:5 explains that the sons of Levi were commanded to receive tithes from the people according to the Law, even though they came out of the loins of Abraham. Scripture further tells us that Levi, the father of the Levitical priesthood who received tithes, also paid tithes through Abraham. The Bible says that because he was in Abraham's loins many generations before he was born, it was accounted unto him as being a tither. Glory to God! The principle of tithing is so strong that it goes through the bloodline as a generational blessing. Our children's children will be blessed for the tithes we pay today. Furthermore, Hebrews 7 reveals to us that in the Levitical priesthood, tithes were received by men who were subject to death (and it would one day cease). But in the case of Melchizedek, they are paid unto one who lives perpetually. What is this saying? Melchizedek represents Jesus. This scripture reminds us of the symbolic representation that when we pay tithes unto Jesus, the One who is eternal, it is something that we do until He returns. Scripture is clearly telling us that we are now paying tithes unto a priesthood that never ends! The principle of tithing was effective before, during, and after the Law. Melchizedek is perpetual, and as long as He exists, we must be obedient in tithing to Him (Jesus). As long as there is a storehouse, we need to bring the tithes to it.

Is tithing relevant for the born-again believer today? What a silly question! It is a principle that is foundational in the kingdom—*one that is eternal!* The church will one day stop having services, but the kingdom has no end!

Jesus told the Pharisees that they paid their tithes but did not do the things that were most important (Matt. 23:23). Later He responded that they should pay their tithes *and* do the weightier things. This is it—in the New Testament Jesus is saying, "You ought to pay your tithes!" Blind Barnamaeus can see this. Let whosoever has an ear, *hear what the Spirit is saying to the church!*

## Chapter 13

# FRIENDLY FIRE

On December 15, 2011, the entire church was commanding the morning on the prayer line. During our prayer time God released a prophetic word through tongues and interpretation. God has used me many times in this way, but the timing and precision of this word took our church to another level.

### Word of the Lord

> Get in place, get in place; get in rank and file, and do not just get in place. But get in your place. Know your place. Know your skills and know your limitations. Let not that which deceived Eve, and even that deceived the devil, deceive you. Be in place in your mind. Be in place in your own minds, I say, for this is the time and the season to be in place. This is the time, for the milk will no longer be around your mouth. For I am taking you to the meat. For the meat will be the portion of the King of kings. Eat not the king's portion, eat of the portion of the Kings of kings. The countenance shall be favor. For this is the time to get under the spout where the glory is coming out, to pull from the covering which is over you. For even I am covering and cleaning the natural and the spirit. For those who have been covered and have faked it until they made it will be revealed through My grace and mercy.
>
> Yes, I am dealing with the religious, the *kritikos*, the

> judgmental, and even those that put their mouth on My prophet. Wash your mouth with the Word and allow the blood to cover your heart. For this is the time where judgment will come quickly and judgment will be a repercussion that boomerangs, and that will come out of your own mouth.
>
> Get under the spout where the glory is coming out. For the Word is mighty, even in thy mouth. Those with the cottonmouth and the milk mouth and the infection of the mouth will be the ones left behind. The eyes of My glory are coming in and will pass those with the chattering piece. They are quick to gossip and backbite. I say that I am dealing with those trivial things that are so small and so minute and so distracting. Be focused, I say, My children. For this is the time to prepare and for you to see, and a time for you to realize and recognize the covering that has come upon you in a new way, and in that sense is getting all the things out that will eat away your foundation. This is the time to be standing firm. Stand and see My salvation. And as you stand and see My salvation, you will know that your foundation shall be sure. And the gifts that are in you will no longer lie dormant; they will no longer lie and drown in need. For your gifts have been drowning out in need because of greed and because of distraction and because of a lack of focus. I say unto you now to be focused, be satisfied, and be full and be who I've called you to be, and I will release a mantle that will really cause you to be promoted from a place of obscurity to a place where I will cause you to shine so that My glory will be noted, and well noted, and well noted in the earth realm in the midst of the heathen, says the Lord

The day after this prophetic word was given, our ministry had a conference. After the Friday night service we were contacted by a homicide detective and notified that one of our intercessors was found dead in the St. John's River. We did not review the word until a week after the funeral, around the first of January 2012. We committed to a twenty-one-day fast during this time.

It was during this fast that enemies were revealed in our camp. While ministering to a member whom we had identified to be struggling in the church, she confessed that another member was conspiring against the ministry. For the purpose of telling this story, I will call this member Ms. C. Ms. C told the struggling member that the doors of Spoken Word Ministries would be closed soon. We later found out that Ms. C had been seeding the minds of many members in the ministry. She was also in constant contact with others who had left the ministry at odds. She had been slanderously making false accusations against the church and our family for years. We knew that Ms. C had a lying spirit and struggled in many areas of her life, but we continued to reach out to her in hope of deliverance.

In January 2012, after many years of ministry to this lady, I had to admit that she was one of the most evil women I had ever met. The spirit that I believe ruled over her head was the *Queen of Hell*. No matter how charitable our church and family were toward Ms. C, she only returned evil for good. The details of the evil that she ministered to our church and family are not important. The only thing that needs to be highlighted is that she worked witchcraft against us unto death. God's exposure of her assignment during the first week of January 2012 led to the exposure of other enemies in our midst. It was a like a spiritual Rubik's Cube. When a few infiltrators were exposed and removed, it brought our members closer together. The prophetic word that was given on December 15 became like marrow to our bones. The part of the word of the Lord that made reference to *the mouth* particularly stirred in our hearts. We received a greater revelation of the power of life and death in the tongue.

## The Power of the Tongue

> Death and life are in the power of the tongue, and those who love it will eat its fruit.
>
> —Proverbs 18:21, nkjv

Because of what we were experiencing as a church, we could not help but focus on the part of the prophetic word that addressed gossipers, backbiters, critical spirits (*kritikos*), and those who put their mouths on God's anointed. We were warned to wash our mouths with the Word and to allow the blood of Jesus to cover our hearts. The Lord allowed us to know that judgment would come quickly as a repercussion of allowing the wrong thing to come out of our mouths. God spoke of *three demonic states of utterance.*

**Cottonmouth**

*Cottonmouth* is another word for a water moccasin. This is one of the meanest snakes that exist. This serpent is very aggressive, attacks without a cause, and strikes to kill. It delivers a painful and potentially fatal bite. It is called *cottonmouth* because it holds its mouth wide open for long periods of time, and all that can be seen is the white inside its mouth. This snake is a strong swimmer and is noted as the world's only semi-aquatic viper.

I have described the cottonmouth in the natural, and based on these things, the spiritual cottonmouth operates in the following ways:

---

- It is a very poisonous spirit that is assigned to minister death.
- It is malicious and heartless and needs no reason to attack; it attacks without a cause. The assignment of this spirit is not hindered by kind deeds.
- It is a very aggressive spirit and is always on the offense.
- This spirit is rooted in gossip, lies, and everything impure that comes from the mouth. It has no control over the death of its tongue.
- It is a water spirit that draws its power from marine spirits and operates under the covering of the Queen of the Coast.

- Because a queen spirit does not operate alone, it forms a threefold cord with the Queen of Heaven (a principality) and the Queen of Hell.

---

Psalm 35:19–28 sums up everything that we need to know about the cottonmouth spirit:

> Let not those who are wrongfully my foes rejoice over me; neither let them wink with the eye who hate me without cause. For they do not speak peace, but they devise deceitful matters against those who are quiet in the land. Yes, they open their mouths wide against me; they say, Aha! Aha! Our eyes have seen it!
>
> You have seen this, O Lord; keep not silence! O Lord, be not far from me! Arouse Yourself, awake to the justice due me, even to my cause, my God and my Lord! Judge and vindicate me, O Lord my God, according to Your righteousness (Your rightness and justice); and let [my foes] not rejoice over me! Let them not say in their hearts, Aha, that is what we wanted! Let them not say, We have swallowed him up and utterly destroyed him. Let them be put to shame and confusion together who rejoice at my calamity! Let them be clothed with shame and dishonor who magnify and exalt themselves over me! Let those who favor my righteous cause and have pleasure in my uprightness shout for joy and be glad and say continually, Let the Lord be magnified, Who takes pleasure in the prosperity of His servant. And my tongue shall talk of Your righteousness, rightness, and justice, and of [my reasons for] Your praise all the day long.

**Milk mouth**

A *milk mouth* refers to a person who is immature in the Lord but who still attempts to usurp unwarranted power through attention. A person with milk mouth is usually anointed with a great future ahead but suffers from the curse of *proskairos* (the temporal) or getting ahead of the timing of God. This person has a zeal, but not according to knowledge. He or she has vision, but because of the immaturity of prophetic eyesight is subject to:

---

- *Spiritual double vision:* This comes from being double-minded and allowing fear to override true faith.
- *Spiritual farsightedness:* Not being able to deal with the present state of where a person is; farsightedness is when a person operates as if they are seasoned and tender in the things of God, when they are still bland and tough.
- *Spiritual nearsightedness:* When a person is blind to what actually is right before them; he or she can foresee the future but is not able to discern the present hour.
- *Spiritually cross-eyed:* To lack focus and attempt to look in so many different directions at the same time.
- *A spiritual lazy eye:* A slothful spirit with heaviness of lids; even spiritual deformity of the eye; no sharpness of vision.
- *Demonic tunnel vision:* A person with milk mouth has clear sight of what is before him or her but has not soaked in the calling of God long enough to have spiritual peripheral vision.

---

**Infectious mouth**

A person with an infectious mouth has spewed so much poison from his or mouth that it has boomeranged back and become a terminal spiritual disease. I found out while writing this chapter that Ms. C literally has an infection in her mouth that antibiotics cannot cure. Her spiritual state manifested in the natural and became a medical condition that doctors could not cure. I pray that Ms. C will repent and that the mercy of God will be her portion so that her life will be spared. As I speak, she cannot be healed because her mouth is spiritually infected and can only be healed by the power of the word of humility and repentance.

The spirit of the infectious mouth is always undergirded with deception and seduction. It is very contagious. Once this spirit is loosed in a congregation, it can spread like wild fire. The only way to put this fire out is:

---

- To remove the individual spreading the contamination
- To minister healing and spiritual inoculation to infected individuals by the Word of God
- To decontaminate the environment that has been contaminated by the cleansing power of the blood of Jesus and the anointing of the Holy Spirit

---

As a part of your continuing boot camp training, turn to Appendix A, "Section 13-1: Friendly Fire, Scriptures in the Mouth," and continue studying the information in our operations guidebook on the topic of the mouth.

## Chapter 14

# THE PETER PRINCIPLE IN THE KINGDOM

SEEKING PROMOTION IS a natural thing. Everyone wants to excel in his or her area of expertise. But recently I ran across a principle that is a warning for being promoted too fast.

I often speak on the Greek term *proskairos*, which means getting ahead of the timing of God. Even promotion must be timely and strategic. The military has an effective system for promotion that ensures soldiers are ready for promotion. The army has a point system that allows so many soldiers to be promoted at one time so that there will not be an overload of chiefs and not enough Indians. The point system is put in place to promote soldiers based on the needs of the army. For example, the army may not need a lot of leadership in the administrative department but have great need in tactical communications. The points for tactical communication specialist will drop, and the administrative slots will have a high-point requirement. The tactical communication specialist will be promoted first because of the need.

Despite the dropping of the points, the soldier has to pass all tests, requirements, and boards to even qualify to take advantage of the low-point requirement. For example, if a soldier's point requirement has dropped, and he has not passed his physical fitness test, a promotion will be denied. Though the need exists for jobs in his or her area of expertise, the soldier must be physically fit and professionally proficient to get the job done.

My understanding of the Peter Principle took the subject of promotion to another level in my mind. Though physical ability and professional proficiency are key factors, timing and calling hold a lot of weight in the formula. Let's take a look at the importance of this principle.

In 1969 Raymond Hull and Laurence Peter wrote a book titled *The Peter Principle.*[1] Their book highlighted a principle that states that in a hierarchically structured administration, people tend to be *promoted up* to their *level of incompetence.* It states that the process of climbing up the ladder can go indefinitely, until a person reaches a rank where he or she is no longer competent. Understanding this principle was the beginning of the answer to many questions I had concerning promotion in ministry. Let's take a look at Psalm 75:6–8:

> For not from the east nor from the west nor from the south come promotion and lifting up. But God is the Judge! He puts down one and lifts up another. For in the hand of the Lord there is a cup [of His wrath], and the wine foams and is red, well mixed; and He pours out from it, and all the wicked of the earth must drain it and drink its dregs.

This particular word *promotion* is *ruwm* in the Hebrew language, and it means to:

---

- Lift up high
- Mount up
- Make taller
- Levy

---

The Word of the Lord is clear concerning promotion. God promotes whom He wants to promote, and in His timing. Promotion does not come from the east or the west (the world or man). It also does not come from the south (the devil), but God is the judge. Promotion comes from the north, which is the secret place of the Lord. This reminds me of the biblical story of Jacob's ladder. The ladder on which Jacob saw the angels descending and ascending sat upon the earth, and the top of it reached heaven (Gen. 28:12). The key word in this passage is *top*. It is *rosh* in Hebrew, and it means, "chief in rank, time and place; head, captain, on high, first, principal, ruler, the beginning."

It is no secret... God demotes some people and promotes others. Whether we understand it or not, He is the judge (*shaphat*) of all promotion. *Shaphat* means:

---

- To pronounce sentence for or against
- To vindicate or punish
- To govern
- To litigate
- To avenge, condemn, defend, execute judgment, plead, reason, rule

---

Putting it in laymen's terms... GOD IS IN CHARGE!

The steps of a good man are ordered by the Lord, and we must allow Him to direct our path, especially concerning promotion. Just as the Peter Principle relates to secular promotion, I believe that it relates to promotion in the kingdom. The cup that Psalm 75:8 speaks of is a cup of God's wrath. It is a terrible thing to become too zealous and overly ambitious in *self-promoting pride*. Proverbs 3:35 says that the wise shall inherit glory, but shame shall be the "promotion of fools" (KJV). This word *shame* (*qalown*) refers to disgrace, confusion, dishonor, and reproach. *Strong's Exhaustive Concordance* also mentions the word *pudenda*, which is a thing to be ashamed of and often relates to the private parts of a man or woman's body.

There are so many scriptures that warn believers to wait on the Lord. Isaiah 49:23 says that those who wait on the Lord shall not be ashamed. Second Corinthians 4:18 explains why we should wait on the Lord.

> Since we consider and look not to the things that are seen but to the things that are unseen; for the things that are visible are temporal (brief and fleeting), but the things that are invisible are deathless and everlasting.

This scripture speaks of things that are unseen. The King James Version of the Bible calls the things that are unseen *temporal.* Temporal is *proskairos* in the Greek and means "getting ahead of the timing of God."

Romans 10:15 says that the feet of those who preach the gospel of Jesus Christ are beautiful. I have recently come to understand that this passage relates to feet that are led by God. The word *beautiful* is *horaios* in the Greek. It is defined as feet that move in season, in the right hour or timing of the Lord.

As believers we are in the world but not of the world. We cannot depend on worldly false promotion to get ahead in life. True promotion only comes from God. The world will present a smoke-screen of false promotion to make things look as though they are not. This kind of promotion is only temporal, and the person eventually ends up farther behind than ahead. Self-exaltation and false promotion are the way of the world. The devil makes it seem as though the wicked always get ahead. Not so! I believe Psalm 37:38: "As for transgressors, they shall be destroyed together; in the end the wicked shall be cut off."

## Obedience Is Better Than Sacrifice

A sure way to be free from the curse of the Peter Principle of the kingdom is to obey the Lord. When I had the dream to run for a key political position in my city, my motivation was not about:

---

- My past experience in the field
- It being my time or season
- My dreams or aspirations to achieve success

---

My motivation was solely rooted in the fact that it was the will of God for me to get in the race. I did not focus on anything other than that. After I came to a conclusion that it was God's will for my life, nothing else mattered—win, lose, or draw!

Running for a political office was never a serious consideration for me. The thought crossed my mind, but I only saw it as just that, *a thought*. To tell you the truth, I did not even know what a city council member's job description was. I had never been to a city council meeting until my first day at work.

It is important to know that when God calls you to do something, NO EXPERIENCE is required. In my autobiography I wrote about how my son Mike Mike went into the NFL with no collegiate experience. He is retired and has a Super Bowl Ring from his championship with the New York Giants. It was hard for him to get into a camp with no allocation. He had the phrase "Allocated by Jesus" on the back of his car window. Just as He did with Mike's NFL miracle, God made a slot for me where there was no allocation. Not only did I have no political experience, but the position I was running for was literally designed for a white, male Republican. I was a black, female blue-dog Democrat, but I was allocated by Jesus!

When I stepped into the race, I let everyone know that God had sent me. Though many did not understand, they cannot deny that my promotion was from the Lord. I was not just running against opponents—I was competing against a system that had been put in place for a long time. I was offered a large sum of money to get out of the race. A group of homosexual racists tried to harass me throughout the entire campaign. The last leg of the race was between me and a not-so-nice opponent. Everyone knew that he had a bad reputation, and his campaign managers attempted to match my troubled past with his very troubled present situation.

I was called all kinds of names, people whispered as I entered campaign venues, and my opponent had almost three times the financial support I had. Publicly no one expected me to win. I was definitely the underdog facing an impossible situation. But behind the scenes God was touching the hearts of people from all kinds of backgrounds to support me. Republicans, Democrats, blacks, whites, young, and old people came out on election night and made a statement that spoke loudly for my favor.

First, I give God all the honor, glory, and praise, but I thank Him for the people in Duval County who voted for me. God used the scripture that declares that the last will be first and the first will be last. My race gave hope to so many people who have been considered last and feel hopeless because of their troubled past. My campaign headquarters did not have any VIPs, media teams, or political personalities on the night of the election. While having a party with my family, church members, friends, and a few supporters, we witnessed a miracle. The polls closed with me leading my opponent by less than two hundred votes. Glory to God! The next day I was announced the official winner with an eleven-hundred-vote lead.

Though I did not have experience, I was equipped. I began to realize that God had been preparing me for the position of City Councilwoman at Large, Group 1 in Jacksonville, Florida, from birth.

I was the first black homecoming queen at the same junior high school where I was a part of race riots in the seventies. I was also the first black president of the student council at the same school. I went to Jean Ribault Senior High School and became homecoming queen and president of the student council there also. To tell the truth, I just took pictures in the yearbook for all four of these positions and was never active in the positions because of distractions in my life. I was not interested in the power of the positions; just breaking the mold of how things had always been was good enough for me. Since I won homecoming queen and president of the student council at Highlands Junior High, young blacks have been holding positions since. Now that's apostolic!

Believe it or not, as the campaign came to an end, I thought that my assignment in the race was to stop a not-so-nice man from holding one of the highest offices in my city. I really could not imagine working in an office in City Hall after traveling the world on a weekly basis. I thought, "How can I trade in first-class plane tickets around the world to sit in an office overlooking the streets I used to play on as a little girl?" The reality of my victory brought a slight fear of the unknown to my heart as I was preparing to be sworn in to public office. I was stepping into a realm that was so unfamiliar to me and about to encounter a new kind of warfare—political power! I knew I could not play the game of politics or be a part of the status quo system. I cried out, "God, how will I fit in?"

Because I stepped out on faith and lifted my right hand as my left hand lay upon a huge Bible, all of heaven backed me up. God is my witness…it was not until I laid my hand on that Bible that I realized…I WAS CALLED! Not just called out of a fast life on the streets, but called to be a gatekeeper in the gates of the same streets. I began to think, "Why not me? This is what the political process is supposed to be about. Real people—representing the people!"

The people of my city did not need another superstar politician. They just needed an empty vessel anointed to lead by God who could fit in the slot. That's me…because God made the mold. As I laid my hand on the Holy Bible, the revelation came to me that God knows all the answers to all the problems in my city, and I will rend my heart and yield my vessel to allow Him to use me as a laborer for the people.

How schizophrenic could our country be to attempt to take prayer out of everything, yet when we sit as witnesses in courtrooms or swear in as elected officials, we do so on the Holy Bible? When I was sworn in on the Bible, I knew that I was in the right place, at the right time, doing the right thing—and no devil in hell could mess with that! Selah.

## The Demon-Buster Is an Elected Official

After being delivered from the race riots of my past, I have never been motivated by the black/white (racial battle) thing. I do not draw lines, because darkness abides in people of all color. At the beginning of my campaign I encouraged people who would not vote for me because I was black. I am proud to be a black American woman, and I feel like I have so much more to offer my city than the color of my skin. When I deal with people, I am very careful not to judge them by the color of their skin but by the content of their character. Trying to explain this to people was like talking to a brick wall. I eventually gave in and decided to accept the fact that people would vote for me for whatever reason they chose, and I would let the work that I did as an elected official speak for me. Winning with almost ninety-three thousand votes was a great start!

I know that a lot of black people voted for me because I am black—it is what it is! I know that there are some people whom I will never please. And the truth is, when you do great things, you will have greater enemies. My prayer is that a few people will see the integrity of Jesus Christ in my life and respect me as a professional and sense my passion to serve the people of my city for real.

The reality of this political chapter in my life is that God cut out a slot for me in the spirit that no one else could fit into. No man-made system, money, gainsayers, naysayers, or soothsayers could stop the plan that God had for me. The only way I could have lost was to defeat myself by disobeying the Master. The political race was not the highlight of my victory. The highlight (for me) was that I knew that I was smack-dab in the middle of God's perfect will. I experienced the manifestation of what we preach about all the time. God has a divine plan for our lives created before the foundation of the earth. We have to get in place to let His kingdom come so that His will can be done.

After the election I ran across some words from the Lord I had written down (in listening prayer) in 1993. In them was a note of a vision I had. I wrote that I saw my face on a political billboard that headlined *Put Prayer Back in Schools!* I do not remember writing this note, but it was in my handwriting, and I was reading it eighteen years after the fact! I never thought twice about the vision. I had received prophetic words about being involved in politics, but it was never the desire of my heart.

*A word of warning:* Be careful not to seek the desires of your heart! Seek the face of the Father and His will, and He will not only give you the desires of your heart, but He also will put the right desires in your heart in the first place. Jesus made His position clear: "Not My will!" Many Christians fear stepping out in the will of God because His will is always rooted in the impossible. Remember, His ways are not our ways, and His thoughts are not our thoughts. God does not give us assignments that are "tiptoe through the tulip" tasks. We are to do greater works than Jesus. The Bible calls them great exploits! These exploits start with the will of God.

I can better explain the will of God by telling about an experience I had with God when I was first saved.

I was standing in the foyer of my apartment in Frankfurt, Germany. I was a staff sergeant in the army at the time. My prayers were being answered so quickly I was concerned. This was not happening with the Christians whom I hung out with. God was answering my prayers in a startling way! It was as if I would have whatever I said. (Does this sound familiar?) I questioned God as to why this was happening for me and not most of my Christian friends. He told me that He was blessing me because I had given up so much so fast. I quit the world cold turkey. I did not take a smooth transition into Christianity by hanging out on the edge until I learned to walk in shallow water. I plunged out into the deep when I could not even swim. I broke every religious rule and did not consider the traditions of men. Though chaos was all around me, God always allowed me to maintain order in my new walk with Him. I did not *just meet Jesus*—a shift had taken place in my generations. It was such a dramatic shift that it affected people, places, and things that I came in contact with.

God also told me that because I did not hesitate to give up anything for Him and had given all my desires to Him, He had put His desires in my heart. He told me that He was not necessarily answering my prayers, but He was manifesting the things that I had allowed Him to put in my heart. This was good enough for me. My ambition became His ambition.

The spirit of fleshy ambition is prevalent in the churches today. People who fall prey to this spirit are transformed from saints to *can'ts* and *ain'ts.*

## Relating the Peter Principle to Ministry

The prophetic ministry can be an example of the Peter Principle in ministry. All believers have the *spirit of prophecy* because it is the testimony of Jesus Christ (Rev. 19:10). Note that because a person has the *gift of prophecy* (1 Cor. 13:2) does not mean that he or she should be in the *office of the prophet* (Eph. 4:11). People haphazardly promote themselves when it comes to the prophetic ministry. This is a dangerous thing.

The Peter Principle warns us to not be anxious for promotion to a possible place of incompetence. I will say this from a spiritual perspective: "On every level there are new devils. Do not take on a mantle or position where you do not have the power to fight off the demons that come with the territory." Because you flow fluently in a gift does not mean that you are to be promoted to the office. Many ministers are out of synchronization with the Holy Spirit because they did well where they were and went to the next level out of the will of God.

Intercession can be another danger zone. God has so many anointed intercessors in the body of Christ. Many of them are accurate seers. The problem comes in when they usurp authority and began to judge the constituted authority God has ordained over them. Intercessors must be careful when they "see" things about their leaders from a critical spirit. They can be correct about what they see concerning the leader but in error in the spirit in which they deal with the situation. Wisdom calls for the intercessor to stand in the gap when leaders have faults. They must also be able to "see" the plan of the enemy to move them from under cover.

If prayer warriors do not take heed, they risk promoting themselves in the Spirit by the realm of the flesh, thereby falling prey to the curse of the Peter Principle.

The results of this error will be:

---

- Disqualification in God's book
- An unfinished course
- Missing the mark of destiny

---

Will I run for reelection or seek a higher position? I have no plans to further my career as an elected official. I believe I am doing well as a council member, but I refuse to be promoted to a place of incompetence. In warfare terms it is called being *territorially out of place*. If you see my name on a ballot in four years, truly the Lord has spoken. Until then I will enjoy serving the people of my city with no strings attached. The decisions I make will not be based on how I am rated in the polls. There is a race that I must finish in life that will determine how I am rated in the Lamb's Book of Life, described by the apostle Paul in 1 Corinthians 9:24–27:

> Do you not know that in a race all the runners compete, but [only] one receives the prize? So run [your race] that you may lay hold [of the prize] and make it yours. Now every athlete who goes into training conducts himself temperately and restricts himself in all things. They do it to win a wreath that will soon wither, but we [do it to receive a crown of eternal blessedness] that cannot wither. Therefore I do not run uncertainly (without definite aim). I do not box like one beating the air and striking without an adversary. But [like a boxer] I buffet my body [handle it roughly, discipline it by hardships] and subdue it, for fear that after proclaiming to others the Gospel and things pertaining to it, I myself should become unfit [not stand the test, be unapproved and rejected as a counterfeit].

# Chapter 15
## GETTING BACK TO OUR ROOTS

In the army every soldier is governed by and expected to adhere to the army regulations that have been set in place by the Department of the Army (DA). DA abides under the governance of the armed forces. Army regulations serve a twofold purpose:

1. To put guidelines in place for all soldiers to adhere to and abide by
2. To provide individual rights for all soldiers

Though soldiers sign up to belong to the military twenty-four hours a day, seven days a week, they have rights. A soldier who does not know his rights may be taken advantage of by a bad leader. In America the Constitution of our country specifically lists our rights as citizens.

There was a time in America when the Pledge of Allegiance, "The Star-Spangled Banner," and the Bill of Rights meant something to every American. Today our children are better at maneuvering through the high technology of computer systems than they are at singing "The Star-Spangled Banner." Mandatory disciplines that were required in schools to assure that we educated a patriotic generation are not considered a priority anymore.

With the onslaught of the neglect of the disciplines that promoted patriotism in our country came the degeneration in the school system of the biblical principles that our country was founded on.

In the boot camp of the Lord we must understand the principle that the Lord spoke of in Luke 16:8. He stated that the "children of this world are in their generation wiser than the children of light" (KJV). For example, we are building edifices and filling them with people when those who are enemies of the gospel are conquering nations. We are growing churches for services, and the enemies of the gospel are taking over the media, writing the laws, and becoming more creative in brainwashing our children with perversion and the occult. We have replaced Bibles with Harry Potter books, and churches are financing abortions by paying for insurances that supply the morning-after pill.

Just like soldiers in the natural army, we have rights as citizens. These rights are called the *Bill of Rights*. The birth of these rights came into existence when the Huguenots fled from France to the Jacksonville, Florida, area for religious liberty.

History indicates that on June 30, 1564, the Huguenots declared a day of Thanksgiving and offered the first Protestant prayer in America at Ft. Caroline on the St. John's River: "We sang a psalm of Thanksgiving unto God, beseeching Him that it would please Him to continue His accustomed goodness toward us."[1]

Some would argue that they only placed a monument (without praying) at Ft. Caroline in 1562 and then settled the territory in 1564. But think about it...just because there was no official record of prayer, it does not mean prayer did not take place. After escaping religious persecution and overcoming the challenges of a rough voyage in 1562, I can only imagine that when Jean Ribault and his crew landed at Ft. Caroline this first time they could not help but at least say, "Thank You, Jesus!"

In his historical account Charles Bennett states: "Ribault sighted the east coast of Florida and on May 1 entered the mouth of a majestic river which he named the River of May (Now the St. John's).

There he landed and prayers were sent heavenward in thanksgiving for safe voyage."[2]

A historical map in the ceiling of the Cox Corridor in the House wing of the Capitol Building in Washington DC titled, "Ft. St. Augustine," displays the dates of three founding cities:

---

- St. Augustine (1565)
- Jamestown (1607)
- Plymouth (1620)

---

These dates commemorate three important dates for the colonization of our great country, but let us not forget the First Coast. If my numbers are correct, 1562 comes before any of the dates listed in the ceiling of the Cox Corridor.

According to Bill Federer's *American Minutes*, in 1989 Rep. Bennett recited the history of Ribault's return to Ft. Caroline in 1564:

> Three small ships carrying 300 Frenchmen led by Rene de Laudonniere anchored in a river known as the St. John's. On June 30, 1564, construction of a triangular shaped fort...was begun with the help of a local tribe of Timucuan Indians...(Ft. Caroline was) home for this hardy group of Huguenots...their strong religious motivation inspired them.[3]

Jacksonville, Florida, sponsored the 450-Year Jean Ribault Celebration on May 1, 2012. Excitement was in the air as historical pictures were unveiled, bands played, and French military ships reenacted the voyage of Jean Ribault to Jacksonville. My prayer is that this monumental celebration will stir the hearts of people of faith to remember the martyrs who lost their lives in this plight for religious liberty and the persecuted churches of today. As the blood of the martyrs of our history cry out from the ground, victory is in the air.

I also thank God for the recent Supreme Court decision for the government to stay out of the affairs of the church. This is what the language (not law) of "separation of church and state" is all about—keeping the state out of the church so there will be no government-controlled religions—not keeping the church out of the state!

To maintain the liberties and protections that God has blessed us with as Americans, we must impart the right principles to the next generation. They must be educated to understand the value of our constitutional rights in America.

My heart is heavy because the children in America today do not have a clue about the true roots of America and how important constitutional rights are. I believe that intercessors must begin to pray over the Bill of Rights, declaring the content out loud and prophetically speaking over these rights, in Jesus's name.

---

## THE BILL OF RIGHTS: AMENDMENTS 1–10 OF THE CONSTITUTION

### Amendment 1

> Congress shall make no law respecting an establishment of religion, or prohibiting the free exercise thereof; or abridging the freedom of speech, or of the press; or the right of the people peaceably to assemble, and to petition the government for a redress of grievances.

This amendment simply states that churches have the right to be free from government control. As long as religions do not practice things like human or animal sacrifices, polygamy, or other acts that are against the law, government intervention into the affairs of the church is illegal. It also emphasizes freedom of speech and freedom of the press. Lastly, this amendment permits peaceful assemblies.

**Amendment 2**

> A well regulated militia, being necessary to the security of a free state, the right of the people to keep and bear arms, shall not be infringed.

This amendment establishes the fact that our country will have a military and gives US citizens the right to own their own weapons.

**Amendment 3**

> No soldier shall, in time of peace, be quartered in any house, without the consent of the owner, nor in time of war, but in a manner to be prescribed by law.

This amendment assures American citizens that their homes will not be forcefully used to house soldiers in the military, during war or peacetime.

**Amendment 4**

> The right of the people to be secure in their persons, houses, papers, and effects, against unreasonable searches and seizures, shall not be violated, and no warrants shall issue, but upon probable cause, supported by oath or affirmation, and particularly describing the place to be searched, and the persons or things to be seized.

This amendment protects citizens from illegal search and seizures of their property.

**Amendment 5**

> No person shall be held to answer for a capital, or otherwise infamous crime, unless on a presentment or indictment of a grand jury, except in cases arising in the land or naval forces, or in the militia, when in actual service in time of war or public danger; nor shall any person be subject for the same offense to be twice put in jeopardy of life or limb; nor shall be compelled in any criminal case to be a witness against himself, nor be deprived of life, liberty, or property, without due process of law; nor shall private property be taken for public use, without just compensation.

**Amendment 6**

> In all criminal prosecutions, the accused shall enjoy the right to a speedy and public trial, by an impartial jury of the state and district wherein the crime shall have been committed, which district shall have been previously ascertained by law, and to be informed of the nature and cause of the accusation; to be confronted with the witnesses against him; to have compulsory process for obtaining witnesses in his favor, and to have the assistance of counsel for his defense.

Amendments 5 and 6 protect citizens from being wrongfully imprisoned. They assure that people cannot be tried twice for the same crime. I also think it is important that these amendments allow people to face their accusers and tell their side of the story.

**Amendment 7**

> In suits at common law, where the value in controversy shall exceed twenty dollars, the right of trial by jury shall be preserved, and no fact tried by a jury, shall be otherwise reexamined in any court of the United States, than according to the rules of the common law.

This amendment affords citizens to have rights to a trial by jury.

**Amendment 8**

> Excessive bail shall not be required, nor excessive fines imposed, nor cruel and unusual punishments inflicted.

This amendment protects citizens from excessive bail and cruel and unusual punishment.

**Amendment 9**

> The enumeration in the Constitution, of certain rights, shall not be construed to deny or disparage others retained by the people.

**Amendment 10**

> The powers not delegated to the United States by the Constitution, nor prohibited by it to the states, are reserved to the states respectively, or to the people.

# PART FOUR

# SPIRITUAL BATTLE STRATEGIES

The soldier in God's army must be prepared to defend the kingdom of God and his or her fellow soldiers from every attack of our enemy, Satan. He or she must prepare for attack by knowing the weaknesses and vulnerabilities not only of self but also of others. He or she must have as a foundation a strong warrior ethos and a winning spirit that permeates his or her life and is expressed by the way he or she reflects the power and courage found through the Holy Spirit.

## A SPIRITUAL WARRIOR ETHOS

- I am a soldier of Jesus Christ.
- I am a warrior and a member of a team. I serve the people of the kingdom of God and live the kingdom's values.
- I will always place the mission first.
- I will never accept defeat.

- I will never quit.
- I will never leave a fallen comrade.
- I am disciplined, spiritually tough, trained, and proficient in my warrior tasks and drills.
- I will always maintain my spiritual weapons and myself.
- I stand ready to engage the enemy and destroy all demonic enemies in close combat.
- I am a guardian of spiritual freedom and the kingdom's abundant life.
- I am a soldier of Jesus Christ.[1]

---

## Chapter 16

# SOLDIERS AGAINST TERRORISM

ONE OF THE greatest wiles of the enemy is to catch us off guard. His main tool is the spirit of terror. This is how our natural enemies come against our country. The spirit of terror manifests itself in natural and spiritual ways. I believe that learning the terms and getting a working knowledge of the enemies of our nation in the natural is a great spiritual discipline. This chapter assignment is to pray against terrorism in America. I have given information in this chapter that will enhance your vocabulary on the subject. Check it out.

To define terror, we must first note that terror is a spirit. It is a spirit that releases intense, overmastering fear, panic, or dread. It manifests as acts or threats of violence with the ultimate goal of intimidating, ruling over, and conquering. The highlight of terror is to catch its target off guard and by surprise. This explains what Psalm 91:5 describes in noting "terror of the night." The enemy wants to creep in when we are unaware or unsuspecting of his attacks. It is a kind of spiritual guerilla warfare. You know the enemy is out there seeking whom he may devour, but the *whens* and *wheres* give power to the terror attack.

> You shall not be afraid of the terror of the night, nor of the arrow (the evil plots and slanders of the wicked) that flies by day.
>
> —PSALM 91:5

God's Word tells us that we perish for a lack of knowledge. To be knowledgeable on any topic, we must increase our vocabulary and be familiar with the words that relate to the subject. In this case my goal is to increase your natural vocabulary on terms that relate to terror. The ultimate goal is to ignite intercession based on what we know, which will ignite intercession on the unknown. This is why people who hold professional positions make great intercessors. They are knowledgeable about the natural aspects of the profession and can allow the Holy Spirit to use their natural authority to tap into new levels of spiritual warfare. For example, a detective who handles homicide crimes will be a great intercessor for a city with a high crime rate. He or she has spiritual and natural authority.

America is the enemy's number one target for terrorism. If it were not for the supernatural hedge of protection that God has put around our country, we would be in trouble. You are about to get a basic training course on how to stand in the gap against terrorism. Terroristic assignments are strategically released against:

---

- Individuals
- Families
- Businesses/organizations
- Visions
- Churches and ministries
- Relationships
- Nations
- Communities

---

We must build beachheads to ward off these attacks through the Word of God. The spearheading anointing attacks and the beachhead anointing builds walls of protection through warfare. A beachhead is not just a wall the keeps the enemy out; it is a garrison of troops that surround the guarded area to destroy anything that attempts to enter. A beachhead is more than a wall; it is a WEAPON!

Therefore we must build our natural vocabulary to understand terroristic terms so that the Holy Spirit can make us sharpshooters of intercession to shut down the plots and plans of every conspiracy meant for evil against us.

| TERRORISM NAMES, TERMS, AND DEFINITIONS | |
|---|---|
| **Abu Sayyaf** | Abu Sayyaf, or "bearer of the sword," is the smaller of two Islamist groups whose goal is to establish an Islamic state in the Southern Philippines. Abu Sayyaf, which split from the Moro National Liberation Front in 1991, has ties to numerous Islamic fundamentalist groups and finances their operations through criminal acts such as kidnapping for ransom, extortion, and piracy; al Qaeda may also contribute funding. Estimates state there are between two hundred and five hundred Abu Sayyaf terrorists.[1] |
| **Afghanistan** | At the time of September 11, 2001, Afghanistan was governed by the Taliban and was the home of Osama bin Laden. After US air strikes, which began on October 7, 2001, President G. W. Bush and the United States pledged more than $300 million in humanitarian aid to Afghanistan. In December 2001 the US embassy in Kabul was opened for the first time since 1989.[2] |
| **agroterrorism** | Terrorist attacks using animal diseases (i.e., anthrax), natural pests (i.e., the potato beetle), molds or other plant diseases, or defoliation agents (i.e., Agent Orange) to destroy crops and thus affect food supply. |

| TERRORISM NAMES, TERMS, AND DEFINITIONS | |
|---|---|
| **air marshal** | A plainclothed, armed federal marshal who flies commercial flights in order to prevent hijackings. The United States started using air marshals, also known as sky marshals, after September 11; however, there are not enough air marshals to go around, so many flights do not have them. |
| **airborne** | Any substance carried by or through the air |
| **al-Gama'a al-Islamiyya (The Islamic Group, IG)** | Islamic radical group that emerged spontaneously during the 1970s after President Sadat released members of the Muslim Brotherhood from prisons throughout Egypt.[3] |
| **al Jazeera** | Satellite television station based in Qatar and that broadcasts throughout the Middle East; it is often dubbed the "CNN of the Arab world." |
| **al Qaeda** | "The Base." An international terrorist group founded in approximately 1989 and dedicated to opposing non-Islamic governments with force and violence. One of the principal goals is to drive the United States armed forces out of the Saudi Arabian peninsula and Somalia by violence. Members of al Qaeda are currently wanted for several terrorist attacks, including those on the US embassies in Kenya and Tanzania as well as the first and second World Trade Center bombings and the attack on the Pentagon.[4] |
| **al Tawhid** | Palestinian terrorist group professing a desire to destroy both Israel and the Jewish people throughout Europe. Eleven al Tawhid were arrested in Germany allegedly as they were about to begin attacking that country.[5] |
| **alpha radiation** | The least penetrating type of nuclear radiation, it is not considered dangerous unless particles enter the body. |

| TERRORISM NAMES, TERMS, AND DEFINITIONS | |
|---|---|
| **American Airlines Flight 11** | En route to Los Angeles from Boston, AA Flight 11 carried eighty-one passengers (including hijackers) and eleven crew. After being hijacked, it crashed into the north tower of the World Trade Center at 8:45 a.m. eastern time on September 11, 2001.[6] |
| **American Airlines Flight 77** | AA Flight 77, with fifty-eight passengers (including hijackers) and six crew members, was en route to Los Angeles from Dulles International Airport. The hijackers crashed the plane into the Pentagon at 9:40 a.m. eastern time on September 11, 2001.[7] |
| **ammonium nitrate-fuel oil (ANFO)** | ANFO is a powerful explosive made by mixing fertilizer and fuel oil; it was used in the first World Trade Center attack as well as in the Oklahoma City bombing. |
| **Armed Islamic Group (GIA)** | Since 1992, after the victory of the Islamic Salvation Front (FIS) in the December 1991 elections was voided, the Armed Islamic Group has sought to overthrow the secular regime in Algeria and replace it with an Islamic state.[8] |
| **assassination** | The murder of a leader of prominent person for political purposes |
| **asymmetric threat** | The use of crude or low-tech methods to attack a superior or more high-tech enemy |
| **Axis of Evil** | Iran, Iraq, and North Korea—called such by President G. W. Bush during his 2002 State of the Union speech as nations that were a threat to US security due to their harboring of terrorists |

| TERRORISM NAMES, TERMS, AND DEFINITIONS | |
|---|---|
| **bin Laden, Osama** | A native of Saudi Arabia, he was the seventh of fifty children of Saudi Arabian builder Mohammed Awad bin Laden. Early in his career Osama helped fight the Soviet Union by recruiting Arabs and building facilities. His hatred of America was based on his views that the United States desecrated holy ground in Saudi Arabia with their presence during the first Gulf War. Expelled from Saudi Arabia in 1991 and from Sudan in 1996, he operated terrorist training camps in Afghanistan. His global network al Qaeda is credited with the attacks on the United States on September 11, 2001, the attack on the USS *Cole* in 2000, and numerous other terrorist attacks.[9] |
| **biochemical warfare** | Collective term for use of both chemical and biological warfare weapons |
| **biochemterrorism** | Terrorism that uses biological or chemical agents as weapons |
| **biological ammunition** | Ammunition, such as a missile warhead or bomb, designed specifically to release a biological agent |
| **biological attack** | An attack involving the deliberate release of germs or other biological substances that cause illness |
| **Biological Weapons Convention (BWC)** | Officially known as the Convention on the Prohibition of Development, Production, and Stockpiling of Bacteriological (Biological) and Toxin Weapons and on Their Destruction, the BWC works toward "general and complete disarmament, including the prohibition and elimination of all types of weapons of mass destruction."[10] |
| **bioterrorism** | The use of biological agents (such as anthrax, ricin, botulism, the plague, smallpox, and tularemia) in a terrorist operation |

| TERRORISM NAMES, TERMS, AND DEFINITIONS | |
|---|---|
| **biowarfare** | The direct or indirect use of biological agents to cause harm to specified population. Direct use involves bringing people into contact with biological agents; indirect use occurs by infecting other animals and plants, which then would cause harm to the population. |
| **blister agents** | Agents causing pain and incapacitation instead of death, thus overloading medical facilities and causing fear in the population when used to injure many people at once |
| **Camp X-Ray** | Internment camp in Guantanamo Bay, Cuba, that was used to house al Qaeda and Taliban prisoners |
| **car bomb** | An automobile used as a bomb to effect death and destruction |
| **carrier** | A source of infection, such as a person or animal, that carries an infectious agent without visible symptoms of disease |
| **cell** | The smallest unit within a guerrilla or terrorist group, generally consisting of two to five people dedicated to the cause. Formation of cells is based on the concept that an apparent "leaderless resistance" makes it hard for counterterrorists to penetrate. |
| **Central Intelligence Agency (CIA)** | US government agency responsible for gathering foreign intelligence |
| **chemical agent** | Toxic substances used to debilitate, immobilize, or kill military or civilian personnel |
| **chemical ammunition** | Munitions, commonly a missile, bomb, rocket, or artillery shell, used to deliver chemical agents |
| **chemical attack** | The intentional release of chemical agents in liquid, gas, or solid form to poison the environment or people |
| **chemical terrorism** | The use of chemical agents such as sarin and VX nerve gas in a terrorist operation |

| TERRORISM NAMES, TERMS, AND DEFINITIONS | |
|---|---|
| **chemical warfare** | The use of toxic chemicals as weapons; chemical warfare does not include the use of herbicides (used to defoliate battlefields) or riot control agents (such as tear gas or mace). |
| **chemical weapons** | Toxic chemical agents such as sarin, VX nerve gas, or mustard gas that produce effects on living targets |
| **choking agent** | Compounds that injure primarily the respiratory tract (i.e., nose, throat, and lungs). Membranes swelling up, lungs becoming filled with liquid, and death resulting from lack of oxygen may occur. |
| **Cipro** | An antibiotic by Bayer that fights inhalation anthrax |
| **counterterrorism** | Measures used to prevent, preempt, or retaliate against terrorist attacks |
| **cruise missile** | A guided missile that flies at a low altitude, following the terrain below it. Examples include Silkworm, Seersucker, and Tomahawks. |
| **cutaneous** | Related to or entering through the skin |
| **cutaneous anthrax** | Anthrax contracted via broken skin; the infection spreads through the bloodstream, causing cyanosis, shock, sweating, and finally death. |
| **cyanide agents** | Colorless liquids inhaled in gaseous form while liquid cyanide and cyanide salts are absorbed by the skin. Symptoms include headache, palpitations, dizziness, and respiratory problems, followed later by vomiting, convulsions, respiratory failure, unconsciousness, and eventually death. Cyanide agents were used by the Nazis in the gas chambers of concentration camps and by Iraq against the Kurds in the 1980s. |
| **cyberterrorism** | Attacks (such as service denial, viruses, or data theft) on computer networks or systems, generally by hackers working with or for terrorist groups |

| TERRORISM NAMES, TERMS, AND DEFINITIONS | |
|---|---|
| **dirty bomb** | Created from radioactive nuclear waste material; when exploded, it causes localized radioactive contamination as the nuclear waste material is carried into the atmosphere, where it is dispersed by the wind. |
| **Ebola hemorrhagic fever (Ebola HF)** | Often fatal in both nonhuman primates and humans. Ebola has appeared sporadically since 1976 when it was first recognized. |
| **e-bomb** | Electromagnetic bomb producing a brief pulse of energy affecting electronic circuitry. At low levels it temporarily disables electronics systems, including computers, radios, and transportation systems. High levels completely destroy circuitry, causing mass disruption of infrastructure while sparing life and property. |
| **ecoterrorism** | Terrorism considered damaging to the environment |
| **Euroterrorism** | Is associated with left-wing terrorism of the 1960s through the 1980s involving the Red Brigade, Red Army Faction, November 17 Group, and other terrorist groups targeting NATO and American interests in Europe.[11] |
| **fallout** | The descent of radioactive particles through the atmosphere as a result of a nuclear explosion; can also refer to the radioactive particles themselves |
| **Fatah** | The political organization created in the 1960s and led by Yasser Arafat. With both a military and intelligence wing, it has carried out terrorist attacks on Israel since 1965. It took over the PLO in 1968. After September 11, 2001, Fatah was blamed for attempting to smuggle 50 tons of weapons into Israel.[12] |
| **fatwa** | A legal opinion or ruling handed down by an Islamic religious leader |

| TERRORISM NAMES, TERMS, AND DEFINITIONS | |
|---|---|
| **Fedayeen Saddam** | Iraq's paramilitary organization loyal to Saddam Hussein's regime and responsible for the use of brutality on civilians who were not loyal to Saddam's policies[13] |

I have devised a prayer against terrorism. Read, study, and pray this prayer. It will ignite a warfare spirit in your soul on the topic and make you more sensitive to the urgency of the situation. I pray that you will get a burden to pray for our nation concerning terrorism. The greatest enemy any armed force has is the one who operates under the guise of guerilla warfare. If you will apply yourself to the information of this chapter, you will become a terror to your enemies.

## Prayer Against Terrorism

*Father, we thank You for the supernatural hedge of protection You have placed around our lives, families, workplaces, businesses, communities, ministries, modes of transportation, and places that we frequent on an everyday basis or on occasion. We lift up local law enforcement agencies, homeland security, transportation security personnel, the FBI, the CIA, the air marshals, and any agencies we have not mentioned that operate as gatekeepers against terrorism. We bind terror by assassination or direct threats against leaders. Agroterrorism is bound and blocked. Our food supply, crops, livestock, or water supply will not be infiltrated. We bind attacks through anthrax, natural pests, mold, or other plant diseases or defoliation agents. All airborne assignments will be blown far away from us in the name of Jesus.*

*We shut down all connections, communications, transmissions, and trafficking that would support every terrorist attack. Let the works of terrorism dry up at the root from the smallest cell group to the largest organization. We destroy the foundation (the base) of al Qaeda operations that oppose our safety and freedom. Let the enemies of Israel be our enemies. We bless those who bless Israel and decree that those who attempt to attack Israel will suffer the repercussions of disobeying the Word of God and attacking the apple of God's eye.*

*We release the angels of the Lord to the Axis of Evil. The threefold cord of Iran, Iraq, and North Korea are severed and has no power. Lord, we thank You for the victory we have received over the strongmen of terrorism. The assignments of the spirits released after the destruction of Osama bin Laden and Saddam Hussein are broken, in Jesus's name.*

*The weapons of warfare of terrorism shall not prosper. Blister agents, car bombs, carriers, chemical agents, chemical attacks, chemical warfare, chemical weapons, sarin, VX nerve gas, choking agents, cruise missiles, cutaneous anthrax, cyanide agents, dirty bombs, e-bombs, fallout, biological attacks of illness, and bioterrorism (anthrax, ricin, botulism, the plague, smallpox, and tularemia) are declared dysfunctional and ineffective.*

*We plead the blood of Jesus over every form of terrorism:*

*Cyberterrorism—attacks against computer networks and other equipment, to include hacking, denial of service attacks, release of viruses or security violations, or theft of data.*

*Ecoterrorism—terrorism that sabotages or damages the environment.*

*Euroterrorism—attacks from European organized groups like the Red Brigade, the Red Army Faction, and the November 17 Group.*

*Biochemterrorism—attacks with the combination of biological and chemical weapons.*

*Biological terrorism—the release of germs that cause illness.*

*Father, we thank You that weapons of mass destruction will be uncovered and removed from the hands of those who desire to bring harm to our nation. We thank You for raising individuals and agencies that will master the creation and activation of counterterrorism in our midst. Amen.*

## Chapter 17

# COMBATING THE SPIRIT OF ERROR

God knows that there are no perfect people, but we can strive to walk in excellence. Instead of *waiting to exhale*, we should be *striving to excel*. Waiting to exhale is what people do when they pattern their lives according to the mandates of the world. Under the control of the prince of the power of the air, they are forced to wait and see what cards will be dealt to them in life. They are bound to play the hand the devil has dealt them, and it is always a losing hand. When we strive to excel, we can do all things through Christ who strengthens us. God has personally dealt our hand, and we cannot lose when we submit to His plan for our lives. A person who strives to excel comes to the knowledge that his or her destiny has been laid out by God. The essence of life is to get in place so that God's perfect will can be fulfilled. This is the root of what excellence is all about.

The opposite of excellence is error. Error does not consist of simple mistakes; it is a place or a road in the spirit. Because of where people are strategically placed in the spirit, natural manifestations come into their lives. Excellence is spirit just as error is. Operating under the spirit of error will cause a person to be out of place with God. There is a road of error and a road of excellence. Being on the right path will automatically combat the spirit of error.

Let's take a look at what the Bible says about the spirit that causes people to err:

- Jesus said that when people do not know the Scriptures or the power of God, it causes them to err (Matt. 22:29).
- Mark teaches that when men do not know Jesus as the living God, they greatly err (Mark 12:27).
- Paul wrote to Timothy that the love of money and coveting leads men to err from the faith and have many sorrows (1 Tim. 6:10).
- Paul also counseled Timothy to know that the lack of studying the Word leads to profane and vain babblings and oppositions of science. These have caused some to err from the faith (1 Tim. 6:15–20).
- In Hebrews we read that when people do not know God's ways, they err in their hearts. This was the case with the children of Israel in the wilderness (Heb. 3:9–10).
- James warns us to avoid lust, which leads to sin, which leads to death (James 1:13–16). Verse 16 sternly warns, "Do not err" (KJV).
- James also reveals that he who converts a sinner from the error of his ways saves a soul from death (James 5:19–20).
- John says that because we are of God and know God, He hears us. This is how we know the spirit of truth in comparison to the spirit of error. When we are not of God and do not know Him, we are open to err (1 John 4:6).

## The Road of Excellence

We must walk out our lives on the road of excellence. We can only *strive to excel* by the leading of the Holy Spirit. *Excel* is the root word for *excellence*. The most important thing to know about excellence is that it is a spirit. God is calling His people to be *in place* to walk in the spirit of excellence.

Please do not get excellence confused with perfection. We will always make mistakes in life. I would like to emphasize the fact that there is a difference between making mistakes and walking in the spirit of error. *We will always make mistakes*, but we do not have to live on the road of error. Error is a road that leads to failure. God has not given us failing spirits. The only way we can be in place with God and fail is to walk in the spirit of fear. God has not given us a spirit of fear but of power, love, and a sound mind. With these attributes we can excel.

*Excellence* is defined as, "the ability to excel; to surpass others and to do extremely well." God has called us to do well at whatever He calls us to do. It is important to understand that where God guides, *He provides*! Through His guidance and provision, we do abundantly above what we can ask or imagine. We do extremely well! We are called to be sons and daughters of excellence.

Walking in the spirit of excellence makes a person refuse to settle for anything less than what God has for them. Nothing upsets me more than to see people who claim to be children of God and joint heirs with Christ who operate on lower levels and substandards to the kingdom. Believers are the light of the world and the salt of the earth. If we do not have a special flavor and if our light does not have a special glow, how can we represent God in the earth?

Do not hold back your God-given talents and gifts because of fears, intimidations, and doubts! The world can be very intimidating if you are sold out to Jesus. So gird up your loins and do not be afraid to be different. Worldly standards have become so normal in the minds of people that our peculiarity (as saints) is becoming more obvious. Be peculiar and proud to be so. Do not be afraid to be different. We are *saints*, not *can'ts* and *ain'ts*.

We are different because we have a different spirit on the inside of us. When you have the Spirit of God on the inside of you, you cannot be like the world. The good news is that being different is the launching pad for your excellence. The Spirit of God on the inside of us ignites the spirit of excellence. The greater one is on the inside of us, and if we get in place, we cannot help but excel.

The world is on a collision course to failure. Without Jesus, everything and anything will fail. But there is no failure in God.

---

- Luke 12:33 says that we should store up for ourselves treasure in heaven that never fail.
- Luke 16:17 says that it is easier for heaven and earth to pass away than for one tittle of the Word of God to fail.
- Luke 21:26 speaks of men's hearts failing them for fear.
- Luke 22:31–32 recounts when Jesus told Peter that the devil wanted to sift him like wheat, but that Jesus had already prayed that Peter's faith would not fail.
- First Corinthians 13:8 teaches that charity never fails.
- Hebrews 1:12 encourages us that our years will never fail.
- Hebrews 12:15 says that if we look after one another diligently, we will not fail to secure the grace of God.

---

Even the people of the world are tired of themselves; they just do not know it yet. Most so-called successful people in the world (who do not know God) struggle with who they really are. People have no choice but to struggle in their personalities when they do not know Jesus. The world is plagued with spirits of competition and jealousy.

Remember that I spoke of error being a road. Just as there is a wrong road, *there is a right path!* The enemy wants us to make excuses that put the blame of our shortcomings on others. The first step in making right paths for ourselves is being responsible for our own shortcomings. No one can make things right in our hearts but us. People can give us advice, pray for us, and even walk us through things, but there is nothing like a made-up mind. We must make up our minds not to struggle with last year's demons.

## Grow *Through* Each Season

Weapons will form in our lives, but they are not supposed to prosper. Some people allow weapons to prosper in their lives when they allow things that they are supposed to be delivered from to flow into their next season. There are seasons when we are assigned to go through things, and when we go through them in the time allotted, *we grow through!* We must learn to tell the devil, "Your season is up in my life!" When we allow the enemy to drag us through the mud with those same-old, same-old problems, they begin to stack up on our emotions.

I have friends who are professional actors and actresses. To be an actor, you have to give yourself totally (mentally and emotionally) into whomever or whatever you are portraying. You must literally become your character and fit into your scene. This is the danger of living the life of drama.

---

- It weighs heavy on your mind and emotions.
- You become the problems you are always dealing with.
- You begin to fit into the scenes that the devil has set up around you.

---

People who live lives of drama never accept responsibility for the things that go wrong in their lives. They spend their days making excuses for their mistakes and slide onto the road of error. I do not believe in bad luck. When bad things plague a person's life, one or all of the three following things are happening:

---

- They are in trouble with God.
- They are under a curse.
- They are on the road of error.

---

When trouble comes, it is not the time to find fault. It is time to seek the face of the Father. Faultfinding and accusing can become a person's daily portion and make that person miserable. Not only is he or she miserable, but *that person also makes everyone around them miserable.* A person who walks in this kind of spirit makes covenant with the accuser of the brethren.

The strongman of the drama is the spirit of litigation. This comes from a warring spirit. There is a difference in being a person of warfare and having a warring spirit. A person with a warring spirit fights when he does not have a legal right to do so. There is a time and a season for everything. There is a time to fight, and there is a time for peace. Dramatic people spend most of their time fighting, whether the time is right or not. Even when a cease-fire is called, they do not get the news and continue to fight, even when the war is over. They simply do not know how to let things go. They carry things around in their hearts, and they lose control of their emotions. The devil holds the reins of their heart. He can push the buttons of drama at his will, and the will of the person is at his beck and call. Some of the signs of the manifestations of the spirit of drama are:

---

- Emotional outbursts in the midst of disputes (often and almost every time)
- Suspicion and the inability to trust
- Insecurity and jealousy of others who excel
- Selfish motives that control the atmosphere with the person's problems always being the highlight
- Fear and rejection that cause the inability to confront and deal with issues
- Generational curses from family members who also lead dramatic lives

- Schizophrenic tendencies that breed from the hypocrisy of trying to hide what is actually going on
- Inability to focus on the important things in life because of dramatic distractions
- Living a defensive, walled life because of the spirits of shame and guilt
- Having failing relationships

---

People who live on the road of drama tread on illegal grounds. They usually go through things that they could have easily avoided or gone around. There are some things that we need to take a detour from and say, "I refuse to go through that!" Hebrews 12:15 warns us to exercise foresight. This means that we should look ahead of the road that we are traveling down. I have avoided many accidents by looking ahead while driving. Another precaution I have used while driving is to stay at least two car lengths behind the car in front of me. In doing this, I avoid getting involved in the accidents of others. The worst kind of accident is the kind with multiple car pileups. I do everything I can to avoid the drama of others. As believers we must be very sensitive to our associations. Just as cars pile up in crashes, when you drive too close to people and their problems, spirits pile up. Their problems can begin to weigh heavily upon your mind. If you socialize or deal with people who have wrong spirits, it will eventually affect you.

I am not suggesting that we must judge or look down on people with struggles in their lives. God wants spiritual troubleshooters to minister to the oppressed. If this is your calling, pray and minister, but be led by God on how you interact. Many believers get heavily burdened by the transference of spirits from the people whom they have ministered to.

## Dealing With the Spirit of Bitterness

> Looking diligently lest any man fail of the grace of God; lest any root of bitterness springing up trouble you, and thereby many be defiled.
>
> —Hebrews 12:15, KJV

The words *looking diligently* are *episkopeo* in the Greek. This is the Greek term for *bishop*, and it means, "to look over with special authority or to supervise." A person with a warring spirit will eventually have roots of resentment, bitterness, and hatred in his or her heart.

God has really been dealing with me about roots this year. I have been spending a lot of time in South Florida. There are trees in the Fort Lauderdale area that have roots that grow outside of the ground and up the tree. Roots are generally below the ground. Even though some may be seen growing slightly above the earth, it's strange to see roots growing up the tree trunk and to the branches.

These externally seen roots remind me of people who have not allowed God to deal with root bondages in their lives. Root bondages are contagious. They start in the heart and spread throughout the body (like roots) to affect every part of a person's life. If we could see in the spirit, we would see people who look like a tree trunk covered with roots wrapped around them. They are so tied up that they cannot move forward in God. The bondage that was once underground (or unseen) is now manifesting in their lives. Examples of root bondages are:

---

- Rejection
- Hatred
- Unforgiveness
- Jealousy

- Bitterness
- Pride
- Violence
- Compulsive lying
- Fear
- Retaliation
- Anger
- Control and possessiveness
- Frustration
- Murder
- Insecurity

---

These root bondages operate through dirty hearts. Roots cannot be sturdy without dirt. Witchcraft works fluently through dirty hearts. This is why Hebrews 12:15 tells us to be supervisors or bishops of our own hearts. In supervising our hearts, we must be sure that the grounds are cleaned. This can only be done through applying the Word of God and the blood of Jesus to our hearts. Weeds of root bondages can choke out the fruit in our lives and leave our grounds barren and hard. Demons seek barren, hard, dry places to plant demonic seeds and spur negativity in our hearts. The result of this is a hard heart. God's remedy for hard hearts (or hearts that cannot be dealt with) is described as breaking up the fallow grounds in the Book of Jeremiah:

> Break up your fallow ground,
> And do not sow among thorns.
> Circumcise yourselves to the Lord,
> And take away the foreskins of your hearts,

> You men of Judah and inhabitants of Jerusalem,
> Lest My fury come forth like fire,
> And burn so that no one can quench it,
> Because of the evil of your doings.
>
> —Jeremiah 4:3–4, NKJV

The heart is the seat of the soul. The Bible tells us that we must break up the fallow ground of our hearts. Jeremiah was prophesying the word of the Lord, and it did not sound like a request; it was a commandment! God was not speaking to the heathens; He was addressing the church. Believers must be responsible for the upkeep of their own hearts. It starts with tilling the hardness of our hearts. Hard hearts make stiff necks. A stiff neck makes us unable to obey God. First Samuel 15:23 refers to a stiff neck as iniquity and relates it to rebellion, which is witchcraft.

Many Christians do not realize that we must be keepers (guardians) of our own heart and soul. This *keeping* does not relate to how God keeps us. It relates to how we must take the initiative to guard and manage our own heart and thought life. Whatever we allow to linger in our minds too long will eventually take root in our hearts. These roots can spread like wild fire until they can be seen by others around us.

We are responsible to weed the grounds of our hearts constantly. We must allow the weed killer of the Word of God to help us keep our hearts and minds right before God. I have a book titled *From a Mess to a Miracle*. I wrote this book because there was a time God had to take my mess and turn it into a miracle. Today I have been saved for almost twenty-two years. My testimony can no longer be *from a mess to a miracle*. I am not saying that I do not have issues in my life; we all do. I am saying that my focus at this point, with my walk with Christ, is to allow God to take me from glory to glory. We have to eventually graduate from our *mess to a miracle* testimonies.

## From Glory to Glory

> And all of us, as with unveiled face, [because we] continued to behold [in the word of God] as in a mirror the glory of the Lord, are constantly being transfigured into His very own image in ever increasing splendor and from one degree of glory to another.
>
> —2 Corinthians 3:18

If I spent my entire life in God focusing on coming out of things, I will never go into what God has for me. The enemy wants us to live in the trail of his demonic dominos. A demonic domino is an order of things that continue to cause other bad things to happen.

For example: A young woman gets pregnant from a married man who denies the child is his. The domino effect of this situation causes her to struggle as a single mother. The rejection the single mother received from the father of her first child leads to two more relationships with men. These relationships lead to two more children being born out of wedlock. When this single mother's oldest child is seventeen years old, the domino effect of everything that has occurred up to this time breeds a bad relationship between the mother and her teenage daughter. The teenage girl starts looking for love in the wrong places. She starts going to nightclubs, staying out all night, and drinking. The domino effect of the empty place in her heart tumbles and ignites a new relationship between her and a twenty-five-year-old man. She is still seventeen. She then looks to this older man as the father figure she never had in her life. The older man is a good person, but this is the deception that makes the teenage girl intentionally get pregnant from him. She moves in with him to get out of her mother's house. Things seem settled for a while, and the dominos stand still. Eventually a domino falls, and the relationship of the now nineteen-year-old girl and her older boyfriend ends. The domino of the generational curse has completed its cycle, and the young girl is now a single mom, just as her mother was.

We must break the demonic dominos or generational curses that flow through our bloodline. I know that they can be broken because I had a similar situation of the young girl used in this analogy. The generational curse has been broken off of me and the lives of my children. Today I have an eighteen-year-old daughter, and she has not started dating yet. The spirits that plagued my life do not plague hers. Through prayer and obedience to God my family has been removed from the reach of the demonic domino. It may fall, but it cannot come nigh my dwelling.

God says that He will take us from one level of glory to the next level of glory in 2 Corinthians 3:18. These levels of glory transfigure us to look more like Christ. Romans, chapter 12, speaks of God's transformation (by the renewing of our minds) in our lives. Transformation changes us on the inside until we begin to change (transfigure) on the outside and look more like Christ. The tree with the roots growing up its trunk represents the counterfeit of what God wants in our lives. These demonic roots make us look more like the devil, but when we allow God to take us from glory to glory, *we look more like Jesus!*

Just as the Word changes us on the inside, it changes us on the outside. We receive this change with unveiled face (no hypocrisy) because we remain in the Word of God.

In order for God to take us to a new level of glory, we must receive the first level of glory. We cannot be distracted by the mess in life that comes to deceive, distract, and detour us from our next level of glory. We can experience an ever-increasing splendor in Christ! Though we will never be perfect, *we are always being perfected!*

## Chapter 18

# GENERATIONAL ENEMIES

OLD TESTAMENT STORIES bring light to what spiritual warfare is all about. The greatest miracles ever experienced by mankind happened during the journey from Egypt to the Promised Land, through the ministry of Moses. Many lessons can be learned from the stories of Moses and the children of Israel.

One of the most beneficial lessons I have learned in my lifetime is that I have enemies who will never be my friends. Not only will these enemies be lifetime foes, but they will also be the enemies of my children's children's children. I call them *generational enemies.*

As I was studying the revelation on generational enemies, I laid my Bible down to get all of my house chores done so I could write this chapter. I was so excited and on fire about what God was speaking to me, I did not want anything to get in the way. Today I am just now writing this chapter—four days later! I received one of the greatest physical attacks that I have ever experienced that day. I was talking to my friend Dr. Fred Hogan on the phone, and something hit me in my eye. I was holding the vacuum cleaner cord in my hand, so my mind told me that I was hit in the eye with the cord. The cord was not retractable, and as I thought about it, hitting myself in the eye with that cord was physically impossible.

As the pain got worse, my eye closed, and I could not see out of it. I was rushed to the emergency room. I knew I had a serious injury when I was rushed ahead of a lobby full of sick people who had been there awhile. After a long period of being hooked up to an IV attached to my eye, the doctor called my husband over to show him what the problem was. The cornea in the center of my eye was cut in the shape of a *V*. The cut was about one-sixteenth of an inch long. This was a very painful experience, but after excellent medical attention, I was released to go home about 3:00 a.m. After getting home, I realized that I had twenty-four hours before I had to get on a plane to travel to a speaking engagement. I called my intercessors to go into overdrive in prayer.

I did not think that it was a coincidence that the devil tried to take my natural eye out at a time when God was revealing so much in the spirit. The good news is that twenty-four hours later I was on a plane to Atlanta to speak at a church. Within a few days my eye was totally healed. The devil should have cut a *D* in my eye (for defeat), because the *V* stood for *victory.*

## The Amalekites

In Numbers 24:20 the Amalekites are called the first among the nations. The word *nations* in this passage is *gowy* in the Hebrew language and means, "the first heathens or enemies of God." Let's take a look at Exodus 17:16:

> And he said, Because [theirs] is a hand against the throne of the Lord, the Lord will have war with Amalek from generation to generation.

Based on Numbers 24:20 and Exodus 17:16, it is clear that the Amalekites have been enemies of God's people from the beginning and will be our enemies forever. As believers we must come to grips with the fact that there are:

- Some people we will never win or please
- Some things that will always war against the righteous
- Some things that God will always war against
- Some agendas of the world that will never submit to the agenda of the kingdom of God

The Amalekites were the direct descendants of Amalek, who was a grandson of Esau. Though Amalek was a close relative of Israel, his descendants are biblically proven to be generational enemies of God's people. Amalek was strategically in position to be the most dangerous kind of enemy to Israel, one of familiarity. The spirit of Amalek is now operating and has always operated under the covering of a familiar spirit or family demon. This is a spirit that operates within close vicinity of the targeted individual or family and travels through the bloodline. Since the encounter with the children of Israel in Exodus 17:8 at Rephidim, Amalek has been assigned against God's anointed. The word *Rephidim* is pronounced *ref-ee-deem* in the Hebrew language and is directly related to *ref-eedaw*, which means, "to be the bottom or back of something as in a chair." It is also related to a Latin word that means, "to sit, recline, or be comfortable." Familiar spirits take advantage of their victims when they become too comfortable.

God gave specific instructions to Saul in 1 Samuel 15:3:

> Now go and smite Amalek and utterly destroy all they have; do not spare them, but kill both man and woman, infant and suckling, ox and sheep, camel and donkey.

It is very important to highlight the word *spare* in this passage of scripture. It is *chamal* in the Hebrew language, and it means, "to have pity or compassion for." In this incident Saul did the exact opposite of what God instructed him to do. He was ordered to *utterly destroy*! Instead he had pity on his enemies, took of the spoils of the battle, and even spared the king of the Amalekites, Agag. He also took the best of the sheep, oxen, fatling, lambs, and all that was good. He only destroyed everything that was undesirable. A lesson that we should learn out of this is that everything that is *good* is not *God*.

Saul became too comfortable in his victory, lay back, and disobeyed God. It is very important to note that 1 Samuel 15:9 states that Saul *and the people* spared Agag. Saul submitted himself to the dictates of the people. I do not believe this is a coincidence. After all, Saul was the people's choice. His kingship was a result of the cries of the people to have a king over them, and those same voices had a demonic influence on how he reigned.

The prophet Samuel rebuked Saul by telling him that obedience is better than sacrifice and that rebellion was as the sin of witchcraft. Saul was so caught up in himself that he could not see that he had disobeyed the Lord:

> Saul said to Samuel, Yes, I have obeyed the voice of the Lord and have gone the way which the Lord sent me, and have brought Agag king of Amalek and have utterly destroyed the Amalekites. But the people took from the spoil sheep and oxen, the chief of the things to be utterly destroyed, to sacrifice to the Lord your God in Gilgal.
>
> —1 Samuel 15:20–21

Saul was blinded by the familiar spirits of the people over whom he was supposed to rule. Verse 26 of the same passage teaches that the Lord rejected Saul as the king of Israel, just as Saul rejected the Word of the Lord. Saul's rebellion not only caused him to lose his kingship, but it also eventually led him into witchcraft and caused his death.

In 1 Samuel 28:14–15 Saul visited a witch to consult a familiar spirit. He consulted a spirit that the Bible says he "perceived" to be Saul. He broke his own rules that he had made about witchcraft and familiar spirits. He even stooped so low as to swear to the witch, in the name of the Lord, that no harm would come to her for conjuring a familiar spirit. As a result he lost everything, even his own life as described in 2 Samuel 1:1–16:

> Now after the death of Saul, when David returned from the slaughter of the Amalekites, he had stayed two days in Ziklag, when on the third day a man came from Saul's camp with his clothes torn and dust on his head. When he came to David, he fell to the ground and did obeisance. David said to him, Where have you come from? He said, I have escaped from the camp of Israel. David said to him, How did it go? Tell me. He answered, The men have fled from the battle. Many have fallen and are dead; Saul and Jonathan his son are dead also.
>
> David said to the young man, How do you know Saul and Jonathan his son are dead? The young man said, By chance I happened to be on Mount Gilboa and I saw Saul leaning on his spear, and behold, the chariots and horsemen were close behind him. When he looked behind him, he saw me and called to me. I answered, Here I am. He asked me, Who are you? I answered, An Amalekite. He said to me, Rise up against me and slay me; for terrible dizziness has come upon me, yet my life is still in me [and I will be taken alive]. So I stood up against him and slew him, because I was sure he could not live after he had fallen. So I took the crown on his head and the bracelet on his arm and have brought them here to my lord.
>
> Then David grasped his own clothes and tore them; so did all the men with him. They mourned and wept for Saul and Jonathan his son, and fasted until evening for the Lord's people and the house of Israel, because of their defeat in battle. David said to the young man who told him, Where are you from? He answered, I am the son of a foreigner, an Amalekite. David said to him, Why were you not afraid to stretch forth your hand to destroy the Lord's anointed? David called one

> of the young men and said, Go near and fall upon him. And he smote him so that he died. David said to [the fallen man], Your blood be upon your own head; for you have testified against yourself, saying, I have slain the Lord's anointed.

The enemy that Saul refused to utterly destroy *eventually destroyed him*. The young man who slew Saul on the battlefield was an *Amalekite*! Saul had the opportunity to cut off his generations. This young man was a generational enemy. Despite all that Saul had done to him, David avenged Saul's death. David asked the young man why he wasn't afraid to stretch his hand against God's anointed. He said that the young man's blood was upon his own head because he testified against himself. David had the young Amalekite killed. He broke the generational curse.

The Amalekites were the first of Israel's human enemies. After receiving manna from the sky and water from the rock, Israel had a much greater need...*deliverance from generational enemies*! The lesson that should be learned from this is that after salvation (coming out of Egypt) and deliverance (going into the Promised Land), there will be enemies to face. The Amalekites you face will do everything to hinder your spirituality. As I stated earlier, Amalek was the grandson of Esau. Esau was the brother who sold his inheritance for a morsel of bread. His belly was his god. The Amalekites will always be assigned to fight our spiritual discipline. These generational enemies hate anything that causes spiritual growth that would enable us to inherit our birthright.

## Jehovah-Nissi

*Jehovah-Nissi* is the name of God that declares the Lord will go before us in battle. Joshua was the captain of the army sent out by Moses to fight the Amalekites. Our operations manual—God's Word—gives a good example of attack of the Amalekites and the supernatural protection of Jehovah-Nissi in the life of Moses and the Israelites.

> And the Lord said to Moses, Pass on before the people, and take with you some of the elders of Israel; and take in your hand the rod with which you smote the river [Nile], and go. Behold, I will stand before you there on the rock at [Mount] Horeb; and you shall strike the rock, and water shall come out of it that the people may drink. And Moses did so in the sight of the elders of Israel. He called the place Massah [proof] and Meribah [contention] because of the faultfinding of the Israelites and because they tempted and tried the patience of the Lord, saying, Is the Lord among us or not?
>
> Then came Amalek [descendants of Esau] and fought with Israel at Rephidim. And Moses said to Joshua, Choose us out men and go out, fight with Amalek. Tomorrow I will stand on the top of the hill with the rod of God in my hand. So Joshua did as Moses said and fought with Amalek; and Moses, Aaron, and Hur went up to the hilltop. When Moses held up his hand, Israel prevailed; and when he lowered his hand, Amalek prevailed. But Moses' hands were heavy and grew weary. So [the other men] took a stone and put it under him and he sat on it. Then Aaron and Hur held up his hands, one on one side and one on the other side; so his hands were steady until the going down of the sun. And Joshua mowed down and disabled Amalek and his people with the sword.
>
> And the Lord said to Moses, Write this for a memorial in the book and rehearse it in the ears of Joshua, that I will utterly blot out the remembrance of Amalek from under the heavens. And Moses built an altar and called the name of it, The Lord is my Banner; And he said, Because [theirs] is a hand against the throne of the Lord, *the Lord will have war with Amalek from generation to generation.*
>
> —Exodus 17:5–16, emphasis added

The people were contending with Moses because they were thirsty. Moses cried unto the Lord because the people were upset to the point of stoning him. Amalek came on the scene *immediately after* the miracle of God that provided the water from the rock. The enemies of God will often launch attacks of backlash and retaliation after a great move of God. Moses told Joshua that he would stand on the top of the hill with the rod of God in his hand.

The word *rod* means, "a branch, a tribe, chastisement or correction, a walking staff to support, a support of life." The rod Moses used represented the authority God had put in his hands. It also represented the presence of God. Moses stood on the hill so that the troops fighting against the enemy could see the rod that he held. The presence of God must be present for victory. Let's take a look at Numbers 14:42–45:

> Go not up, for the Lord is not among you, that you be not struck down before your enemies. For the Amalekites and the Canaanites are there before you, and you shall fall by the sword. Because you have turned away from following after the Lord, therefore the Lord will not be with you. But they presumed to go up to the heights of the hill country; however, neither the ark of the covenant of the Lord nor Moses departed out of the camp. Then the Amalekites came down and the Canaanites who dwelt in that hill country and smote the Israelites and beat them back, even as far as Hormah.

When Moses held the rod of God, not only did it symbolize authority, but it also symbolized being in right standing with God. Numbers 42:43 states that God was not with them in battle because they turned away from Him. The Word of the Lord is clear that they *presumed* to go to battle, but neither the ark of the covenant nor Moses went with them. The Israelites who fought this battle were shamefully defeated, because the presence of the Lord was not with them.

Godly leadership in battle is essential. Every army needs a commander in chief. Moses was more than a general; he was the commander in chief. He had the wisdom and authority to lead the people in battle as God led him. The body of Christ will have more victory in warfare than ever before when our leaders get in place. I believe that sin in the camp will cause defeat in the church. This was so at the battle of Ai. Even a mighty warrior like Joshua could not win victory over a little country like Ai because of the accursed thing in the midst of God's camp. Just as the presence of God brings victory, the accursed thing brings defeat. Joshua presumptuously went after Ai in battle. Samson presumptuously tried to defeat the Philistines as he had before, but he did not know that the presence of the Lord had left him and his strength was gone. King Saul attempted to operate in his kingdom as he always had, never realizing that the Spirit of God had left him.

The word *presumed* in Numbers 14:44 is *aphal* in the Hebrew language, and it means, "to swell up and be lifted up." In other words, when God's people presumptuously go ahead of Him in battle, it is a result of pride. Moses never got ahead of God when leading his people in battle. For example:

- *Healing*—When the children of Israel rebelled against God and snakes bit them, Moses lifted up the rod with the snake for them to look upon to receive healing.
- *Deliverance*—When the Egyptians were gaining on the children of Israel and they were trapped by the Red Sea, Moses stretched the rod of God over the waters.
- *Victory*—When the magicians of Egypt threw their rods on the floor and they became serpents, Moses threw his rod. It also turned into a serpent but devoured the snakes of the magicians.
- *The Greater One in us*—When the Amalekites opposed the Israelites at Mount Horeb, God's people had victory when the rod was held up, and they suffered defeat when Moses's arms were too tired to hold the rod up.

I have heard many teachings on how Moses's arms were held up and caused victory at Mount Horeb. The focus of the messages was always on Moses's arms *when the focus should have been on the rod.* Moses built an altar that he named *Jehovah-Nissi*, which means, "the Lord is my banner and He goes before me in battle."

In the illustration of Moses lifting up the brazen serpent on the pole, the word *pole* means "banner." In the Old Testament banners were not flags like we have in our churches today; the rod of God went before His people in victory—*Jehovah-Nissi*!

I would like for you to conclude your study of generational enemies from this chapter by reading Isaiah 13:2–6 aloud. This is a chapter of great victory in warfare, because the Lord goes before us in battle:

> Raise up a signal banner upon the high and bare mountain, summon them [the Medes and Persians] with loud voice and beckoning hand that they may enter the gates of the [Babylonian] nobles. I Myself [says the Lord] have commanded My designated ones and have summoned My mighty men to execute My anger, even My proudly exulting ones [the Medes and Persians]—those who are made to triumph for My honor. Hark, the uproar of a multitude in the mountains, like that of a great people! The noise of the tumult of the kingdoms of the nations gathering together! The Lord of hosts is mustering the host for the battle. They come from a distant country, from the uttermost part of the heavens [the far east]—even the Lord and the weapons of His indignation—to seize and destroy the whole land. Wail, for the day of the Lord is at hand; as destruction from the Almighty and Sufficient One [Shaddai] will it come!

## Conclusion

# SPIRITUAL BOOT CAMP FINAL WORD

I COULD NOT CLOSE the chapters of this book without giving a tribute to a true soldier of the army of God, James Bailey. I know that he is in heaven basking in the glory of the Lord. There will not be another "Brother James" Bailey.

James died in December 2011, and even as I am writing this chapter, the cause of his death has not been identified. I do not have to know the cause of death to know that he is living eternally in Christ. I have never met anyone who loved Jesus more. I used to joke that James would overdose on the Word if he was not careful. Every time you saw him, he was listening to the Word or trying to give a word. He was what I call a *word-monger.*

James was a soldier in God's army. Many people saw his testimony on *The 700 Club* and have an idea of the life he came out of, but there was so much more. James never told me about his past life, outside of the fact that he served eighteen years of his adult life in prison and he had been on drugs. I met James eight years ago and witnessed his zeal for the Lord every time I saw him.

Many did not know that James was one of the best baseball players in the nation. He played with some of the great names, like Darryl Strawberry, but he was detoured from his career because of drugs. His father was the first black man to have a mechanical contracting license in heating and air conditioning in the state of Florida. He was the owner of JJ Bailey Air Conditioning and Heat.

James lost his mother in 1999 and his father in 2007, but the legacy of his lineage goes on. He has four boys from his wife, Denice Bailey, and an adult son and daughter who recently gave birth to James's twin grandchildren.

I could call on James at any time, and he was there. He almost single-handedly put up hundreds of signs for my campaign around the entire city. He died with the keys to everything that I owned in his pocket. He made the name *servant* have more meaning.

James, I know that you are one of the cloud of witnesses. You are where I am trying to get. God bless your soul, and I am proud to have called you son!

Finally, I would like to say that at the end of 2011, the editor of this book and my family both experienced the greatest loss a parent could imagine, the loss of a child. No matter what the age of the child, you can never imagine what it is like until you experience it firsthand. I know I speak on the behalf of my editor and her family in saying that no matter what you go through in this life, God's grace is sufficient for you. Only God's mercy and grace allowed us to finish this project (both of us having lost a child during the process).

No matter what comes our way, my husband and I are committed to stay on the wall. I encourage you to stay enlisted in the army of the Lord until you meet the commander in chief face-to-face. Do not allow the things you go through or the cares of this world make you go AWOL—FINISH YOUR TOUR OF DUTY!

Jesus is Lord!

—PASTOR KIM

# Appendix A

# YOUR SPIRITUAL OPERATIONS GUIDEBOOK TRAINING PRINCIPLES

THE EXCERPTS IN this section from your spiritual operations guidebook—the Word of God—are the expanded training principles to be studied as directed in this field manual. Read and study each section as you are directed to them in the preceding chapters of the manual.

---

## SECTION 2-1
## SPIRITUAL READINESS

Read this section related to the importance of valor to the soldier in God's army as your expanded study assignment from chapter 2. Let these passages permeate your spirit man. Pray a prayer of decree and declaration that lines up with the content of these scriptures. Allow God to soak you in the vision of being a mighty man or woman of valor. This spiritual exercise will give you a new boldness to obey God.

### 1. Evidence of the superiority of God's valor

#### *Valor in heaven*

> Now war arose in heaven, Michael and his angels fighting against the dragon. And the dragon and his angels fought back, but he was defeated, and there was no longer any place for them in heaven. And the great dragon was thrown down, that ancient serpent, who is called the devil and Satan,

> the deceiver of the whole world—he was thrown down to the earth, and his angels were thrown down with him. And I heard a loud voice in heaven, saying, "Now the salvation and the power and the kingdom of our God and the authority of his Christ have come, for the accuser of our brothers has been thrown down, who accuses them day and night before our God. And they have conquered him by the blood of the Lamb and by the word of their testimony, for they loved not their lives even unto death.
>
> —REVELATION 12:7–11, ESV

> In the beginning was the Word, and the Word was with God, and the Word was God. He was in the beginning with God. All things were made through him, and without him was not any thing made that was made. In him was life, and the life was the light of men. The light shines in the darkness, and the darkness has not overcome it.
>
> —JOHN 1:1–5, ESV

> And that night the angel of the LORD went out and struck down 185,000 in the camp of the Assyrians. And when people arose early in the morning, behold, these were all dead bodies.
>
> —2 KINGS 19:35, ESV

> The LORD goes out like a mighty man, like a man of war he stirs up his zeal; he cries out, he shouts aloud, he shows himself mighty against his foes.
>
> —ISAIAH 42:13, ESV

***The valor of Jesus***

> Jesus answered him, "You would have no authority over me at all unless it had been given you from above. Therefore he who delivered me over to you has the greater sin."
>
> —JOHN 19:11, ESV

***Heavenly valor in man***

> Oh grant us help against the foe, for vain is the salvation of man! With God we shall do valiantly; it is he who will tread down our foes.
>
> —PSALM 108:12–13, ESV

## 2. Examples of biblical men and women of valor

### *Samson*

> Now the house was full of men and women. All the lords of the Philistines were there, and on the roof there were about 3,000 men and women, who looked on while Samson entertained. Then Samson called to the LORD and said, "O Lord GOD, please remember me and please strengthen me only this once, O God, that I may be avenged on the Philistines for my two eyes." And Samson grasped the two middle pillars on which the house rested, and he leaned his weight against them, his right hand on the one and his left hand on the other. And Samson said, "Let me die with the Philistines." Then he bowed with all his strength, and the house fell upon the lords and upon all the people who were in it. So the dead whom he killed at his death were more than those whom he had killed during his life.
>
> —JUDGES 16:27–30, ESV

### *David*

> And the women sang to one another as they celebrated, "Saul has struck down his thousands, and David his ten thousands."
>
> —1 SAMUEL 18:7, ESV

> And David inquired of the LORD, "Shall I pursue after this band? Shall I overtake them?" He answered him, "Pursue, for you shall surely overtake and shall surely rescue."
>
> —1 SAMUEL 30:8, ESV

> And David struck them down from twilight until the evening of the next day, and not a man of them escaped, except four hundred young men, who mounted camels and fled.
>
> —1 SAMUEL 30:17, ESV

> And David took from him 1,700 horsemen, and 20,000 foot soldiers. And David hamstrung all the chariot horses but left enough for 100 chariots.
>
> —2 SAMUEL 8:4, ESV

After this David defeated the Philistines and subdued them, and David took Metheg-ammah out of the hand of the Philistines. And he defeated Moab and he measured them with a line, making them lie down on the ground. Two lines he measured to be put to death, and one full line to be spared. And the Moabites became servants to David and brought tribute. David also defeated Hadadezer the son of Rehob, king of Zobah, as he went to restore his power at the river Euphrates. And David took from him 1,700 horsemen, and 20,000 foot soldiers. And David hamstrung all the chariot horses but left enough for 100 chariots. And when the Syrians of Damascus came to help Hadadezer king of Zobah, David struck down 22,000 men of the Syrians. . . . [Continue reading in your operations guidebook, the Bible.]

—2 SAMUEL 8:1–18, ESV

And David arose and went with all the people who were with him from Baale-judah to bring up from there the ark of God, which is called by the name of the LORD of hosts who sits enthroned on the cherubim. And they carried the ark of God on a new cart and brought it out of the house of Abinadab, which was on the hill. And Uzzah and Ahio, the sons of Abinadab, were driving the new cart, with the ark of God, and Ahio went before the ark. And David and all the house of Israel were celebrating before the LORD, with songs and lyres and harps and tambourines and castanets and cymbals. And when they came to the threshing floor of Nacon, Uzzah put out his hand to the ark of God and took hold of it, for the oxen stumbled. . . . [Continue reading in your operations guidebook.]

—2 SAMUEL 6:2–23, ESV

And David made a name for himself when he returned from striking down 18,000 Edomites in the Valley of Salt.

—2 SAMUEL 8:13, ESV

Blessed be the LORD, my rock, who trains my hands for war, and my fingers for battle.

—PSALM 144:1, ESV

### *Solomon*

"Now therefore as the LORD lives, who has established me and placed me on the throne of David my father, and who has made me a house, as he promised, Adonijah shall be put to death today." So King Solomon sent Benaiah the son of Jehoiada, and he struck him down, and he died.

—1 KINGS 2:24, ESV

### *Elijah*

But Elijah answered the captain of fifty, "If I am a man of God, let fire come down from heaven and consume you and your fifty." Then fire came down from heaven and consumed him and his fifty. Again the king sent to him another captain of fifty men with his fifty. And he answered and said to him, "O man of God, this is the king's order, 'Come down quickly!'" But Elijah answered them, "If I am a man of God, let fire come down from heaven and consume you and your fifty." Then the fire of God came down from heaven and consumed him and his fifty.

—2 KINGS 1:10–12, ESV

### *Rahab*

But Rahab the prostitute and her father's household and all who belonged to her, Joshua saved alive. And she has lived in Israel to this day, because she hid the messengers whom Joshua sent to spy out Jericho.

—JOSHUA 6:25, ESV

### *The Israelites*

And the LORD said to Joshua, "Do not fear and do not be dismayed. Take all the fighting men with you, and arise, go up to Ai. See, I have given into your hand the king of Ai, and his people, his city, and his land. And you shall do to Ai and its king as you did to Jericho and its king. Only its spoil and its livestock you shall take as plunder for yourselves. Lay an ambush against the city, behind it." So Joshua and all the fighting men arose to go up to Ai. And Joshua chose 30,000 mighty men of valor and sent them out by night. And he commanded them, "Behold, you shall lie in ambush against the city, behind it. Do not go very far from the city, but all of you remain ready. And I and all the people who are with me will approach the city. And when they come out against us just as before, we shall flee before them. . . ." [Continue reading in your operations guidebook.]

—JOSHUA 8:1–35 ESV

From the Gadites there went over to David at the stronghold in the wilderness mighty and experienced warriors, expert with shield and spear, whose faces were like the faces of lions and who were swift as gazelles upon the mountains.

—1 CHRONICLES 12:8, ESV

Then Amaziah assembled the men of Judah and set them by fathers' houses under commanders of thousands and of hundreds for all Judah and Benjamin. He mustered those twenty years old and upward, and found that they were 300,000 choice men, fit for war, able to handle spear and shield. He hired also 100,000 mighty men of valor from Israel for 100 talents of silver.

—2 CHRONICLES 25:5–6, ESV

When you go out to war against your enemies, and see horses and chariots and an army larger than your own, you shall not be afraid of them, for the LORD your God is with you, who brought you up out of the land of Egypt. And when you draw near to the battle, the priest shall come forward and speak to the people and shall say to them, "Hear, O Israel, today you are drawing near for battle against your enemies: let not your heart faint. Do not fear or panic or be in dread of them, for the Lord your God is he who goes with you to fight for you against your enemies, to give you the victory."

—DEUTERONOMY 20:1–4, ESV

**2. Instructions for becoming a man or woman of valor**

You shall chase your enemies, and they shall fall before you by the sword. Five of you shall chase a hundred, and a hundred of you shall chase ten thousand, and your enemies shall fall before you by the sword.

—LEVITICUS 26:7–8, ESV

Blessed is the nation whose God is the LORD, the people whom he has chosen as his heritage! The LORD looks down from heaven; he sees all the children of man; from where he sits enthroned he looks out on all the inhabitants of the earth, he who fashions the hearts of them all and observes all their deeds. The king is not saved by his great army; a warrior is not delivered by his great strength. . . . [Continue reading in your operations guidebook.]

—PSALM 33:12–22, ESV

Let every person be subject to the governing authorities. For there is no authority except from God, and those that exist have been instituted by God. Therefore whoever resists the authorities resists what God has appointed, and those who resist will incur judgment. For rulers are not a terror to good conduct, but to bad. Would you have no fear of the one who is in authority? Then do what is good, and you will receive his approval, for he is God's servant for your good. But if you do wrong, be afraid, for he does not bear the sword in vain. For he is the servant of God, an avenger who carries out God's wrath on the wrongdoer. Therefore one must be in subjection, not only to avoid God's wrath but also for the sake of conscience. . . . [Continue reading in your operations guidebook.]

—ROMANS 13:1–14, ESV

But you are a chosen race, a royal priesthood, a holy nation, a people for his own possession, that you may proclaim the excellencies of him who called you out of darkness into his marvelous light. Once you were not a people, but now you are God's people; once you had not received mercy, but now you have received mercy.

—1 PETER 2:9–10, ESV

## SECTION 5-1
## THE GREATEST GIFT—LOVE

### THE IMPORTANCE OF LOVE

This section will show you the importance of love to the soldier in God's army. Although God gives many gifts to His soldiers, the most important of His gifts is love—the love He has shown to you and the love He expects you to show to others.

> But God has so adjusted (mingled, harmonized, and subtly proportioned the parts of) the whole body, giving the greater honor and richer endowment to the inferior parts which lack [apparent importance], so that there should be no division or discord or lack of adaptation [of the parts of the body to each other], but the members all alike should have a mutual interest in and care for one another. And if one member suffers, all the parts [share] the suffering; if one member is honored, all the members [share in] the enjoyment of it. Now you [collectively] are Christ's body and [individually] you are members of it, each part severally and distinct [each with his own place and function]. So God has appointed some in the church [for His own use]: first apostles (special messengers); second prophets (inspired preachers and expounders); third teachers; then wonder-workers; then those with ability to heal the sick; helpers; administrators; [speakers in] different (unknown) tongues. Are all apostles (special messengers)? Are all prophets (inspired interpreters of the will and purposes of God)? Are all teachers? Do all have the power of performing miracles? Do all possess extraordinary powers of healing? Do all speak with tongues? Do all interpret? But earnestly desire and zealously cultivate the greatest and best gifts and graces (the higher gifts and the choicest graces). And yet I will show you a still more excellent way [one that is better by far and the highest of them all—love]. If I [can] speak in the tongues of men and [even] of angels, but have not love (that reasoning, intentional, spiritual devotion such as is inspired by God's love for and in us), I am only a noisy gong or a clanging cymbal.
>
> —1 CORINTHIANS 12:24–31; 13:1

## SECTION 5-2
## THE GREATEST GIFT—LOVE

### THE PRINCIPLES OF THE UNITY OF LOVE

His intention was the perfecting and the full equipping of the saints (His consecrated people), [that they should do] the work of ministering toward building up Christ's body (the church), [that it might develop] until we all attain oneness in the faith and in the comprehension of the [full and accurate] knowledge of the Son of God, that [we might arrive] at really mature manhood (the completeness of personality which is nothing less than the standard height of Christ's own perfection), the measure of the stature of the fullness of the Christ and the completeness found in Him.

So then, we may no longer be children, tossed [like ships] to and fro between chance gusts of teaching and wavering with every changing wind of doctrine, [the prey of] the cunning and cleverness of unscrupulous men, [gamblers engaged] in every shifting form of trickery in inventing errors to mislead. Rather, let our lives lovingly express truth [in all things, speaking truly, dealing truly, living truly]. Enfolded in love, let us grow up in every way and in all things into Him Who is the Head, [even] Christ (the Messiah, the Anointed One). For because of Him the whole body (the church, in all its various parts), closely joined and firmly knit together by the joints and ligaments with which it is supplied, when each part [with power adapted to its need] is working properly [in all its functions], grows to full maturity, building itself up in love....

Therefore, rejecting all falsity and being done now with it, let everyone express the truth with his neighbor, for we are all parts of one body and members one of another. When angry, do not sin; do not ever let your wrath (your exasperation, your fury or indignation) last until the sun goes down. Leave no [such] room or foothold for the devil [give no opportunity to him]. Let the thief steal no more, but rather let him be industrious, making an honest living with his own hands, so that he may be able to give to those in need. Let no foul or polluting language, nor evil word nor unwholesome or worthless talk [ever] come out of your mouth, but only such [speech] as is good and beneficial to the spiritual progress of others, as is fitting to the need and the occasion, that it may be a blessing and give grace (God's favor) to those who hear it.

And do not grieve the Holy Spirit of God [do not offend or vex or sadden Him], by Whom you were sealed (marked, branded as God's own, secured) for the day of redemption (of final deliverance through Christ from evil and the consequences of sin). Let all bitterness and indignation and wrath (passion, rage, bad temper) and resentment (anger, animosity) and quarreling (brawling, clamor, contention) and slander (evil-speaking, abusive or blasphemous language) be banished from you, with all malice (spite, ill will, or baseness of any kind). And become useful and helpful and kind to one another, tenderhearted (compassionate, understanding, loving-hearted), forgiving one another [readily and freely], as God in Christ forgave you.

—EPHESIANS 4:12–16, 25–32

---

## SECTION 6-1
## GOOD COMMON SENSE

### PRAYER TERMS AND PRACTICES TO IDENTIFY

This section contains a listing of the different terms and practices by which you, God's soldier, can develop a vital prayer strategy that will keep you focused on the will and Word of God—for your personal life and for the teaching and instruction of others.

1. *Intercessory prayer*—to make intercession by standing in the gap between a person, place, or thing and the devil
2. *The prayer of the watchman*—to get on the wall and pray concerning the needs of the place surrounded by the wall of prayer. This type of prayer usually comes with a prophetic discernment or apostolic discretion to sound the alarm when trouble is approaching. The prayer watchman is like a spiritual alarm system.
3. *The prayer of agreement*—prayer where power is multiplied by more than one person. One can put one hundred to flight; but two, ten thousand.

4. *Fasting and prayer*—this kind of prayer deals with stubborn spirits and difficult situations. It also takes the prayer warrior to another level of discipline and dedication.
5. *Prayer of petition*—God knows what you need, but He wants you to let Him know what you need through prayers from your heart. This creates a closer relationship with Him.
6. *The sinner's prayer*—the prayer that is prayed by the lost to repent of sins and connect with God for soul salvation.
7. *Confession of faith* (*declarations and decrees*)—prayers of authority that repeat what God has said using the power of life and death in your tongue. These are words that God has already spoken, but when you repeat them with boldness, it shakes the gates of hell.
8. *Confessional prayer* (*repentance of sins*)—if you humble yourself, turn from your wicked ways, and repent of your sins, God will hear from heaven and heal the land. The land includes every area of your life that affects you.
9. *Corporate prayer*—the prayer anointing that comes on the multitude when the people of God fitly joined together tap into the vein of God and pray prayers that bring heaven down to earth.
10. *Listening prayer*—this defines the times when you get quiet before the Lord and allow Him to speak to your spirit man or through you to others through prophetic words. This yielding of yourself to God allows the Holy Spirit to write His will through you.
11. *Warfare prayer*—offensive and defensive prayers that are used as a spiritual weapon against spiritual attacks.
12. *The Nehemiah prayer*—a prayer given to God to ask Him to have no mercy on enemies. This prayer asks God to allow the reproach meant for the person praying to come upon the head of the enemy because he has tried to stop the work of the Lord or provoked Him.

13. *Prayer and meditation*—a quiet time of prayer when you wholly give your mind to God.
14. *Deliverance prayer*—the ministry of inner healing or casting out devils that sets captives free.
15. *Prophetic prayer*—prayer that is given by the unction of the Holy Spirit to speak forth the oracles of God.
16. *A house of prayer* (Matt. 21:13)—a church or group dedicated to the ministry of prayer.
17. *Prayer of faith* (Matt. 21:22)—the prayer that pleases God based on belief in His word.
18. *The early-riser prayer* (Mark 1:35)—prayer that takes place in the early hours of the morning, usually before sunrise.
19. *The prayer of forgiveness* (Mark 11:25)—prayer that moves the blockage of unforgiveness from a person's heart.
20. *The Lord's Prayer*—the biblical prayer given as a guideline in Matthew 6. It tells us how and how not to pray.
21. *The hour of prayer* (Acts 3:1)—a designated time that prayer is ignited.
22. *To tarry in prayer* (Luke 24:49)—the act of praying and waiting on God as an individual or corporately.
23. *The prayer of thanksgiving* (Eph. 1:16)—the gate-opening prayer whereby you begin prayer by thanking God for what He already has done and is about to do.
24. *The prayer wall* (1 Thess. 3:9–10)—organized prayer that is made night and day, usually by a dedicated group of people.
25. *Targeting warfare prayer*—prayer that spearheads, targets, and penetrates the particular areas needed.
26. *The prayer ministry of laying on of hands*—prayers of impartation, casting out devils, ministry of the elders, prophecy, healing, and other

transferences as ministers activate the congregation based on the Word that has been preached.

27. *Inner healing prayer*—ministry to the deepest parts of the hearts of men that destroys lingering emotional and mental residual bondages.
28. *The Macedonian prayer* (Acts 16:9)—a call for ministerial assistance from a ministry in need.
29. *Praying in the Spirit*—a spiritual prayer language that results from the infilling of the Holy Spirit. This kind of prayer gives revelation, ignites spiritual gifts, instills boldness, and strengthens a person against temptation.
30. *Interpretation of tongues*—A gift of the spirit that allows a person to understand and give the interpretation to an utterance of an unknown tongue.

---

## SECTION 6-2
## GOOD COMMON SENSE

### PRAYER PRINCIPLES FROM SPECIFIC SCRIPTURES

1. Pray for those who spitefully use you and persecute you (Matt. 5:44).
2. Do not pray as hypocrites (Matt. 6:5).
3. Enter into your prayer closet and pray to the Father in secret, and the Father will reward you openly (Matt. 6:6).
4. Do not pray vain, repetitious prayers as the heathens do: to be seen; to get what they can get out of it; to exalt the things of the world and the realm of the flesh (Matt. 6:7).
5. There are some things that will not be dealt with except by fasting and prayer (Matt. 17:21).
6. Do not make long prayers as the scribes and hypocrites, because this releases a greater damnation (Matt. 23:14).

7. Pray that you will not enter into temptation; the spirit is willing but the flesh is weak (Matt. 26:41).
8. Jesus said that He could have called down twelve legions of angels (Matt. 26:53).
9. The harvest is great but the laborers are few; pray for the Lord of the harvest to send laborers (Luke 10:2).
10. Always pray and do not faint (Luke 18:1).
11. Jesus prayed that our faith would not fail and that once we were converted, we would strengthen our brethren (Luke 22:32).
12. Jesus told His disciples to stop sleeping and pray lest they enter into temptation (Luke 22:46).
13. Jesus prayed for God to send the Holy Ghost (John 14:16).
14. Jesus is the greatest intercessor that there ever was (John 16:26).
15. We should pray for God to set leaders in place because He knows their heart (Acts 1:24).
16. We should pray that the end-time church will continue in the apostles' doctrine, fellowship, the breaking of bread, and prayer. This is the prayer that increases churches (Acts 2:42).
17. We should pray for people to be filled with the Holy Ghost. Biblically they should speak in tongues, prophesy, and speak with boldness (Acts 4:31).
18. Believers are called to give themselves continually to prayer and the ministry of the Word (Acts 6:4).
19. Believers should be set in ministry by prayer and the laying on of hands by the elders (Acts 6:5–6).
20. Believers whose hearts are not right should repent of their sins and pray that God would forgive them for the thoughts of their hearts (Acts 8:21).

21. Simon the sorcerer asked Peter to pray to the Lord for him, that the things Peter had spoken over him would not come to pass (Acts 8:24).
22. Cornelius (a centurion) was a devout Christian who feared God, gave generously to people, and always prayed to God (Acts 10:1–2).
23. Prayer and offerings come before God as a memorial (Acts 10:4).
24. Cornelius was fasting and praying when an angel appeared to him (Acts 10:30).
25. Peter fell into a trance while praying (this is when he received the revelation of salvation to the Gentiles) (Acts 11:5).
26. Prayer without ceasing was made for Peter to be released from prison (Acts 12:5).
27. The spirit of python is assigned to follow ministries and mock true prayer (Acts 16:16).
28. There is power in the midnight cry (prayer at midnight) (Acts 16:25).
29. Without ceasing, Paul made mention of the Romans in prayer (Rom. 1:9).
30. The Spirit makes intercession for us with groanings that cannot be uttered (Rom. 8:26).
31. Paul prayed for Israel to be saved, because they had zeal but not according to knowledge (Rom. 10:1–2).
32. Paul prayed certain prayers by permission and not of commandment based on his association or knowledge of the situation (1 Cor. 7:5–6).
33. It is scriptural to pray for the interpretation of tongues (1 Cor. 14:13).
34. When we pray in unknown tongues, the Spirit prays through us, but we do not understand what we are praying unless God gives the interpretation (1 Cor. 14:14).
35. We should pray (in tongues) with understanding and without understanding (1 Cor. 14:15).

36. As ambassadors for Christ we should pray for people to be reconciled to God (2 Cor. 5:20).
37. We must watch as well as pray (Eph. 6:18).
38. Prayer petitions must be made with joy (Phil. 1:4).
39. We are commanded to avoid being anxious in all situations, but in all situations with prayer and supplication and with thanksgiving make our requests known unto God (Phil. 4:6).
40. Petitions must be made to God so that *doors of utterance* will be opened to speak the mysteries of Christ (Col. 4:3).
41. As we remember the works of people, we should make mention of them in our prayer (1 Thess. 1:2).
42. The prayer for sanctification (1 Thess. 5:17–23): pray without ceasing; in everything give thanks; quench not the Spirit; despise not prophesying; prove all things and hold fast to good; abstain from evil appearance; the God of peace will sanctify you wholly; your spirit, soul and body will be preserved blameless unto the coming of the Lord.
43. Petitions must be made unto God so that His Word will have free course (2 Thess. 3:1).
44. As we lift our hands in prayer, it should be without wrath or doubt (1 Tim. 2:8).
45. We should pray with our conscience free of impurity. Repentance of sins is a prayer prerequisite (2 Tim. 1:3).
46. The elders of the church are called to pray for the sick (James 5:13–14).
47. The effectual, fervent prayer of the righteous produces great results (James 5:16).
48. God is no respecter of persons; He respects effectual, fervent prayer (Acts 10:34; James 5:16–17).

49. The prayers of husbands can be hindered if they do not honor their wives; unto whom much is given much is required (1 Pet. 3:7).
50. Gods eyes are on the righteous, and He hears their prayers, but His face is against them that do evil (1 Pet. 3:12).
51. We are commanded to be sober and to watch as well as pray (1 Pet. 4:7).
52. Praying in the Holy Ghost builds spiritual strength (Jude 20).
53. The prayers of the saints come before God out of the hand of angels (Rev. 8:4).

---

## SECTION 8-1
## DO NOT BE WEARY IN WELL-DOING

### ISAIAH 40

Comfort, comfort My people, says your God. Speak tenderly to the heart of Jerusalem, and cry to her that her time of service and her warfare are ended, that [her punishment is accepted and] her iniquity is pardoned, that she has received [punishment] from the Lord's hand double for all her sins. A voice of one who cries: Prepare in the wilderness the way of the Lord [clear away the obstacles]; make straight and smooth in the desert a highway for our God! Every valley shall be lifted and filled up, and every mountain and hill shall be made low; and the crooked and uneven shall be made straight and level, and the rough places a plain. And the glory (majesty and splendor) of the Lord shall be revealed, and all flesh shall see it together; for the mouth of the Lord has spoken it.

A voice says, Cry [prophesy]! And I said, What shall I cry? [The voice answered, Proclaim:] All flesh is as frail as grass, and all that makes it attractive [its kindness, its goodwill, its mercy from God, its glory and comeliness, however good] is transitory, like the flower of the field. The grass withers, the flower fades, when the breath of the Lord blows upon it; surely [all] the people are like grass. The grass withers, the flower fades, but the word of our God will stand forever. O you who bring good tidings to Zion, get up to the high mountain. O you who bring good tidings to Jerusalem, lift up your voice with strength, lift it up, be not afraid; say to the cities of Judah, Behold your God! Behold, the Lord God will come with might, and His arm will rule for Him. Behold, His reward is with Him, and His recompense before Him. He will feed His flock like a shepherd: He will gather the lambs in His arm, He will carry them in His bosom and will gently lead those that have their young.

Who has measured the waters in the hollow of his hand, marked off the heavens with a [nine-inch] span, enclosed the dust of the earth in a measure, and weighed the mountains in scales and the hills in a balance? Who has directed the Spirit of the Lord, or as His counselor has taught Him? With whom did He take counsel, that instruction might be given Him? Who taught Him the path of justice and taught Him knowledge and showed Him the way of understanding?

Behold, the nations are like a drop from a bucket and are counted as small dust on the scales; behold, He takes up the isles like a very little thing. And all Lebanon's [forests] cannot supply sufficient fuel, nor all its wild beasts furnish victims enough to burn sacrifices [worthy of the Lord]. All the nations are as nothing before Him; they are regarded by Him as less than nothing and emptiness (waste, futility, and worthlessness). To whom then will you liken God? Or with what likeness will you compare Him? The graven image! A workman casts it, and a goldsmith overlays it with gold and casts silver chains for it.

He who is so impoverished that he has no offering or oblation or rich gift to give [to his god is constrained to make a wooden offering, an idol; so he] chooses a tree that will not rot; he seeks out a skillful craftsman to carve and set up an image that will not totter or deteriorate. [You worshipers of idols, you are without excuse.] Do you not know? Have you not heard? Has it not been told you from the beginning? [These things ought to convince you of God's omnipotence and of the folly of bowing to idols.] Have you not understood from the foundations of the earth? It is God Who sits above the circle (the horizon) of the earth, and its inhabitants are like grasshoppers; it is He Who stretches out the heavens like [gauze] curtains and spreads them out like a tent to dwell in, Who brings dignitaries to nothing, Who makes the judges and rulers of the earth as chaos (emptiness, falsity, and futility).

Yes, these men are scarcely planted, scarcely are they sown, scarcely does their stock take root in the earth, when [the Lord] blows upon them and they wither, and the whirlwind or tempest takes them away like stubble. To whom then will you liken Me, that I should be equal to him? says the Holy One. Lift up your eyes on high and see! Who has created these? He Who brings out their host by number and calls them all by name; through the greatness of His might and because He is strong in power, not one is missing or lacks anything. Why, O Jacob, do you say, and declare, O Israel, My way and my lot are hidden from the Lord, and my right is passed over without regard from my God? Have you not known? Have you not heard? The everlasting God, the Lord, the Creator of the ends of the earth, does not faint or grow weary; there is no searching of His understanding. He gives power to the faint and weary, and to him who has no might He increases strength [causing it to multiply and making it to abound].

Even youths shall faint and be weary, and [selected] young men shall feebly stumble and fall exhausted; but those who wait for the Lord [who expect, look for, and hope in Him] shall change and renew their strength and power; they shall lift their wings and mount up [close to God] as eagles [mount up to the sun]; they shall run and not be weary, they shall walk and not faint or become tired.

---

## SECTION 13-1
## FRIENDLY FIRE

### SCRIPTURES IN THE MOUTH

Blessings are upon the head of the [uncompromisingly] righteous (the upright, in right standing with God) but the mouth of the wicked conceals violence.

—PROVERBS 10:6

The mouth of the [uncompromisingly] righteous man is a well of life, but the mouth of the wicked conceals violence.

—PROVERBS 10:11

Wise men store up knowledge [in mind and heart], but the mouth of the foolish is a present destruction.

—PROVERBS 10:14

The mouths of the righteous (those harmonious with God) bring forth skillful and godly Wisdom, but the perverse tongue shall be cut down [like a barren and rotten tree].

—PROVERBS 10:31

The lips of the [uncompromisingly] righteous know [and therefore utter] what is acceptable, but the mouth of the wicked knows [and therefore speaks only] what is obstinately willful and contrary.

—PROVERBS 10:32

With his mouth the godless man destroys his neighbor, but through knowledge and superior discernment shall the righteous be delivered.

—PROVERBS 11:9

By the blessing of the influence of the upright and God's favor [because of them] the city is exalted, but it is overthrown by the mouth of the wicked.

—PROVERBS 11:11

The words of the wicked lie in wait for blood, but the mouth of the upright shall deliver them and the innocent ones [thus endangered].

—PROVERBS 12:6

From the fruit of his words a man shall be satisfied with good, and the work of a man's hands shall come back to him [as a harvest].

—PROVERBS 12:14

A man shall eat good by the fruit of his mouth: but the soul of the transgressors shall eat violence.

—PROVERBS 13:2, KJV

He who guards his mouth keeps his life, but he who opens wide his lips comes to ruin.

—PROVERBS 13:3

In the fool's own mouth is a rod [to shame] his pride, but the wise men's lips preserve them.

—PROVERBS 14:3

The tongue of the wise utters knowledge rightly, but the mouth of the [self-confident] fool pours out folly.

—PROVERBS 15:2

The mind of him who has understanding seeks knowledge and inquires after and craves it, but the mouth of the [self-confident] fool feeds on folly.

—PROVERBS 15:14

A man has joy in making an apt answer, and a word spoken at the right moment—how good it is!

—PROVERBS 15:23

The mind of the [uncompromisingly] righteous studies how to answer, but the mouth of the wicked pours out evil things.

—PROVERBS 15:28

Divinely directed decisions are on the lips of the king; his mouth should not transgress in judgment.

—PROVERBS 16:10

The mind of the wise instructs his mouth, and adds learning and persuasiveness to his lips

—PROVERBS 16:23

The appetite of the laborer works for him, for [the need of] his mouth urges him on.

—PROVERBS 16:26

The words of a [discreet and wise] man's mouth are like deep waters [plenteous and difficult to fathom], and the fountain of skillful and godly Wisdom is like a gushing stream [sparkling, fresh, pure, and life-giving].

—PROVERBS 18:4

A [self-confident] fool's lips bring contention, and his mouth invites a beating.

—PROVERBS 18:6

A [self-confident] fool's mouth is his ruin, and his lips are a snare to himself.

—PROVERBS 18:7

A worthless witness scoffs at justice, and the mouth of the wicked swallows iniquity.

—PROVERBS 19:28

Food gained by deceit is sweet to a man, but afterward his mouth will be filled with gravel.

—PROVERBS 20:17

He who guards his mouth and his tongue keeps himself from troubles.

—PROVERBS 21:23

The mouth of a loose woman is a deep pit [for ensnaring wild animals]; he with whom the Lord is indignant and who is abhorrent to Him will fall into it.

—PROVERBS 22:14

Wisdom is too high for a fool; he opens not his mouth in the gate [where the city's rulers sit in judgment].

—PROVERBS 24:7

Like the legs of a lame man which hang loose, so is a parable in the mouth of a fool.

—PROVERBS 26:7

Like a thorn that goes [without being felt] into the hand of a drunken man, so is a proverb in the mouth of a [self-confident] fool.

—PROVERBS 26:9

The slothful and self-indulgent buries his hand in his bosom; it distresses and wearies him to bring it again to his mouth.

—PROVERBS 26:15

A lying tongue hates those it wounds and crushes, and a flattering mouth works ruin.

—PROVERBS 26:28

Let another man praise you, and not your own mouth; a stranger, and not your own lips.

—PROVERBS 27:2

This is the way of an adulterous woman: she eats and wipes her mouth and says, I have done no wickedness.

—PROVERBS 30:20

If you have done foolishly in exalting yourself, or if you have thought evil, lay your hand upon your mouth.

—PROVERBS 30:32

Open your mouth for the dumb [those unable to speak for themselves], for the rights of all who are left desolate and defenseless.

—PROVERBS 31:8

Open your mouth, judge righteously, and administer justice for the poor and needy.

—PROVERBS 31:9

She opens her mouth in skillful and godly Wisdom, and on her tongue is the law of kindness [giving counsel and instruction].

—PROVERBS 31:26

---

# Appendix B

# BOOT CAMP STUDY NOTES

In the military the core vision of training is to teach every soldier to lead. In times of war there is always the possibility of casualties. If the leader becomes a casualty, the next person in charge has to be prepared to take the baton and complete the mission. We must have generational resources that cause us to endure.

## Basic Training in Our American Roots

It is difficult to complete a mission without understanding the blueprint of the original vision. We cannot be spiritual leaders in America without having a revelation of the founding blueprint of our country. When embarking on the topic of leadership as believers, we should be made aware of our American roots. These questions must be asked:

---

1. Is America a Christian nation?
2. Did the first presidents of America consider God when carrying out the duties of their public office?
3. Did the Founding Fathers of America relate Christianity to government?

4. Who were the key martyrs recorded in American history who died for the gospel of Jesus Christ?
5. Who were the biblical martyrs noted in biblical history?

---

Today Americans have been deceived by obscure statements such as "the separation of church and state." Not only is it deceiving, but it is also unconstitutional. The Founding Fathers had no intention of keeping the church out of state business. They wanted to keep the state out of church business. This is the foundation our country was built upon. Most of the Founding Fathers based the decisions they made for this country on biblical principles. They also staked the future of the United States of America on its citizens' ability to govern themselves under the kingship of Jesus Christ.

Review the information given on the leaders in this lesson, and then answer the questions following.

**The Supreme Court of the United States of America**

In 1892, in the case of the *Church of the Holy Trinity v. United States*, the Supreme Court examined thousands of documents concerning the founding of the nation, including every state constitution as well as compacts leading up to the time of the American Revolution. After ten years of research the court issued a unanimous decision that included the recognition that not only is this nation historically and culturally religious, but also that the very system of government and our laws are based on a Christian worldview.

Regarding this documentary evidence, the court further stated:

> There is *no dissonance* in these declarations. There is a universal language pervading them all, having *one meaning*. They affirm and reaffirm that *this is a religious nation*. These are not individual sayings, declarations of private persons. They are organic utterances. They speak the *voice of the entire*

> *people....*This is a religious people....*This is a Christian nation.*[1]

There has been debate about whether America can truly be called *a Christian nation*. But there is no doubt—from looking at historical records—that the founders and citizens of America were committed to Christian ideals. They were grateful to God for His guidance and set out to create a better nation, one that was built on biblical principles. At a time when other nations were rejecting Christianity (such as France during the French revolution of 1789), America stood out as an example of faith and optimism.

Historical events and statements contributed to the spiritual roots of our country.

**Continental Congress**

Victory over British forces at Saratoga (October 1777) led to this order by George Washington declaring the first National Proclamation of Thanksgiving.

> For as much as it is indispensable duty of all men to adore the superintending providence of Almighty God—to acknowledge with gratitude their obligation to him for benefits received, and to implore such further blessings as they stand in need of—And it having pleased him in his abundant mercy, not only to continue to us the innumerable bounties of his common providence, but also to smile upon us in the prosecution of a just and necessary war, for the defense and establishment of our unalienable rights and liberties....It is therefore recommended...to set apart Thursday, the 18th day of December next, for solemn Thanksgiving and praise.[2]

**Congress of the United States**

On September 25, 1789, Elias Boudinot introduced a resolution for a public day of thanksgiving and prayer:

> That a joint committee of both Houses be directed to wait upon the President of the United States, to request that he would recommend to the people of the United States a day of public thanksgiving and prayer to be observed by acknowledging, with grateful hearts, the many signal favors of Almighty God, especially by affording them an opportunity peaceably to establish a Constitution of government for their safety and happiness.[3]

Below I have listed quotes from leaders in American history that prove what the spiritual atmosphere was really like in the hearts and minds of our Founding Fathers. These quotes from the first presidents of our nation are very clear that they did not separate their faith from their political positions:

**George Washington—the first president of the United States**

Washington's retirement into private life was proceeded by this excerpt from his farewell address on September 19, 1796:

> Of all the dispositions and habits which lead to political prosperity, religion and morality are indispensable supports. In vain would that man claim the tribute of patriotism who should labor to subvert these great pillars of human happiness.[4]

Washington commented on the course of the Revolutionary War. The instances of divine intervention were seen and noted in the American press as well as British papers.

> The hand of Providence has been so conspicuous in all this, that he must be worse than an infidel who lacks faith, and more than wicked, who has not gratitude enough to acknowledge his obligations.[5]
>
> —George Washington

Washington's private prayer was recorded near his headquarters on the Hudson River. Washington also wrote many of his own prayers in his field notebook.

> And now, Almighty Father, if it is Thy holy will that we shall obtain a place and name among the nations of the earth, grant that we may be enabled to show our gratitude for Thy goodness by our endeavors to fear and obey Thee.[6]

**John Adams—the second president of the United States**

Long before the Revolutionary War made America an independent nation, John Adams wondered what kind of land might be built if the Bible were taken seriously and its principles honestly practiced.

> Suppose a nation in some distant region should take the Bible for their only law-book, and every member should regulate his conduct by the precepts there exhibited! Every member would be obliged, in conscience, to temperance and frugality and industry; to justice and kindness and charity towards his fellow men; and to piety, love, and reverence, towards Almighty God... What a Eutopia; what a Paradise would this region be![7]
>
> —Diary entry,
> February 22, 1756

In a letter to Zabdiel Adams, dated June 21, 1776, John Adams wrote:

> Statesmen, my dear Sir, may plan and speculate for liberty, but it is religion and morality alone, which can establish the principles upon which freedom can securely stand. The only foundation of a free constitution is pure virtue; and if this cannot be inspired into our people in a greater measure than they have it now, they may change their rulers and the forms of government, but they will not obtain a lasting liberty.[8]

Many leaders at the time of the American Revolution saw America as an opportunity to set up a better country, one based on biblical values.

**Thomas Jefferson—the third president of the United States**

> God who gave us life gave us liberty. Can the liberties of a nation be secure when we have removed a conviction that these liberties are the gift of God?[9]
>
> —Inscribed on a panel on the Jefferson Memorial in Washington DC

Men and nations tend to forget the goodness of God. The founders warned that America would lose its liberty if it did not honor God.

> Who can proclaim the mighty acts of the Lord
> or fully declare his praise?
> Blessed are they who maintain justice,
> who constantly do what is right.
>
> —Psalm 106:2–3, NIV

**James Madison—the fourth president of the United States**

> We have all been encouraged to feel in the guardianship and guidance of that Almighty Being whose power regulates the destiny of nations.[10]
>
> —First Inaugural Address, March 4, 1809

**James Monroe—the fifth president of the United States**

> The liberty, prosperity and happiness of our country will always be the object of my most fervent prayer to the Supreme Author of All Good.[11]
>
> —Second Inaugural Address, March 5, 1821

Public prayer in Congress existed from the beginning. Prayers for the nation were never viewed as purely private but were often made publicly for public servants and the nation as a whole.

**John Quincy Adams—the sixth president of the United States**

> Is it not that, in the chain of human events, the birthday of the nation is indissolubly linked with the birthday of the Savior? That it forms a leading event in the progress of the gospel dispensation? Is it not that the Declaration of Independence first organized the social compact on the foundation of the Redeemer's mission upon the earth? That it laid the cornerstone of human government upon the first precepts of Christianity, and gave to the world the first irrevocable pledge of the fulfilment of the prophecies, announced directly from Heaven at the birth of the Savior and predicted by the greatest of the Hebrew prophets six hundred years before?[12]
>
> —Independence Day speech,
> July 4, 1837

**Andrew Jackson—the seventh president of the United States**

> That Book [the Bible], sir, is the rock on which our republic rests.[13]
>
> —Andrew Jackson,
> June 8, 1865

The Bible was seen as vital to the foundation of the nation.

**Abraham Lincoln—the sixteenth president of the United States**

Lincoln issued a proclamation appointing a national day of prayer and fasting. An excerpt reads:

> It is the duty of nations as well as of men to own their dependence upon the overruling power of God, to confess their sins and transgressions in humble sorrow, yet with assured hope that genuine repentance will lead to mercy and pardon,

> and to recognize the sublime truth, announced in the Holy Scriptures and proven by all history, that those nations only are blessed whose God is the Lord.[14]

There were other Founding Fathers who were very open about their faith in the political arena. It is amazing to know how much they affected why our country is the strong force it is today, along with their strong faith in God.

**Benjamin Rush—signer of the Declaration of Independence, founder of the first anti-slavery society in America**

> I have alternately been called an Aristocrat and a Democrat. I am neither. I am a Christocrat.[15]

Rather than rule by elite (aristocracy) or rule by the many (democracy), many of the first Americans preferred *rule by Christ.*

**William Bradford—governor of Plymouth Colony**

> Last and not least, they cherished a great hope and inward zeal of laying good foundations, or at least making some ways toward it, for the propagation and advance of the gospel of the kingdom of Christ in the remote parts of the world, even though they should be but stepping stones to others in the performance of so great a work.[16]

America was colonized by Christians whose aims included the spread of the gospel.

**John Hancock—first to sign the Declaration of Independence**

In the days leading up to the Revolutionary War, circumstances looked grim. Many leaders called on the citizenry to fast and pray for America, as did John Hancock with these opening remarks:

> In circumstances dark as these, it becomes us, as Men and Christians, to reflect that whilst every prudent measure

> should be taken to ward off the impending judgments...all confidence must be withheld from the means we use; and reposed only on that God rules in the armies of Heaven, and without His whole blessing, the best human counsels are but foolishness.[17]
>
> —Proclamation for Day of Fasting, Humiliation and Prayer, April 15, 1775

**John Witherspoon—president of the College of New Jersey (Princeton)**

Just prior to the Declaration of Independence and the ensuing war, the Continental Congress called for a National Day of Fasting, Humiliation, and Prayer. John Witherspoon followed up with a speech at the College of New Jersey (later called Princeton):

> While we give praise to God, the Supreme disposer of all events, for His interposition on our behalf, let us guard against the dangerous error of trusting in, or boasting of, an arm of flesh.[18]

**Alexis de Tocqueville—a French statesman and historian**

De Tocqueville observed and wrote about America beginning in 1831. As a Frenchman he may be regarded as an outside, objective witness to the Christian nature of early America.

> In the United States the sovereign authority is religious...there is no country in the world where the Christian religion retains a greater influence over the souls of men than in America, and there can be no greater proof of its utility and of its conformity to human nature than that its influence is powerfully felt over the most enlightened and free nation of the earth.[19]

> America is great because it is good, and if America ever ceases to be good, America will cease to be great.[20]

**Gouverneur Morris—delegate to the Constitutional Convention; writer of the final draft of the Constitution**

> Religion is the only solid basis of good morals; therefore education should teach the precepts of religion, and the duties of man towards God.[21]

Public education and Christianity were seen as working together, not conflicting.

> The fear of the LORD is the beginning of wisdom, and the knowledge of the Holy One is understanding.
>
> —PROVERBS 9:10, NKJV

**John Jay—the first chief justice of the Supreme Court, coauthor of *The Federalist Papers***

> Providence has given to our people the choice of their rulers, and it is the duty, as well as the privilege and interest, of our Christian nation to select and prefer Christians for their rulers.[22]

> Unto Him who is the author and giver of all good, I render sincere and humble thanks for his manifold and unmerited blessings, and especially for our redemption and salvation by His beloved Son.[23]

Many founders fervently believed that God was the final source of both mercy and judgment.

**Benjamin Franklin—statesman, author, scientist, and printer**

When the Constitutional Convention was deadlocked and it looked like it might be dissolved by disagreements, Franklin called the delegation to prayer with these words:

> I have lived, Sir, a long time, and the longer I live, the more convincing proofs I see of this truth—*that God governs in*

> *the affairs of men.* And if a sparrow cannot fall to the ground without his notice, is it probable that an empire can rise without his aid?[24]

America's founders recognized God's guidance throughout every aspect of the nation's formation.

**Roger Sherman—signer of all four of the major founding documents**

In a speech to Congress Roger Sherman said:

> Admiring and thankfully acknowledging the riches of redeeming love, and earnestly imploring that divine assistance which may enable us to live no more to ourselves, but to him who loves us and gave himself to die for us.[25]

Many founders understood that the gift of salvation requires people to respond in selfless ways.

**Alexander Hamilton—signer of the Constitution**

Hamilton referred to the Constitution when he said:

> For my own part, I sincerely esteem it a system, which, without the finger of God, never could have been suggested and agreed upon by such a diversity of interests.[26]

Without God's guidance, many people with such different interests could not have agreed upon the principles by which America was to be governed.

**Jedediah Morse—educator and geographer**

> Whenever the pillars of Christianity shall be overthrown, our present republican forms of government, and all the blessings which flow from them, must fall with them.[27]

### Samuel Adams—cousin to John Adams; called the Father of the American Revolution

> We have this day restored the Sovereign to whom all men ought to be obedient. He reigns in heaven and from the rising to the setting of the sun, let His kingdom come.[28]
>
> —Upon signing of the Declaration of Independence

Samuel Adams saw God as the only true King of the nation. The Declaration of Independence was seen as a way of restoring God to His rightful place in the hearts of Americans. Its signing was the reverse of what the early Hebrew republic had done in calling for a kind of rejecting God in 1 Samuel 8:4–7.

> The rights of the colonists as Christians... may be best understood by reading and carefully studying the institutes of the great Law Giver and Head of the Christian Church, which are to be found clearly written and promulgated in the New Testament.[29]

### Joseph Story—justice to the Supreme Court

> There is not a truth to be gathered from history, more certain, or more momentous, than this, that civil liberty cannot long be separated from religious liberty without danger, and ultimately without destruction to both. Wherever religious liberty exists, it will, first or last, bring in, and establish political liberty.[30]

### Daniels Webster—politician, diplomat, and educator

> Finally, let us not forget the religious character of our origin. Our fathers were brought hither by their high veneration for the Christian religion. They journeyed by its light, and labored in its hope. They sought to incorporate its principles with the elements of their society, and to diffuse its influence through all their institutions, civil, political, or literary. Let us cherish these sentiments, and extend this influence still more widely; in

the full conviction that that is the happiest society which partakes in the highest degree of the mild and peaceful spirit of Christianity.[31]

—Speech at the bicentennial of the Pilgrims' landing at Plymouth Rock, December 22, 1820

## Patrick Henry—member of the Continental Congress

Whether this [new government] will prove a blessing or a curse, will depend upon the use our people make of the blessings which a gracious God hath bestowed on us. If they are wise, they will be great and happy. If they are of contrary character, they will be miserable. Righteousness alone can exalt them as a nation. Reader! Whoever thou art, remember this, and in thy sphere practice virtue thyself, and encourage it in others.[32]

—Back of Stamp Act Resolves, May 1765

## William Prescott—commander of the colonial militia at Bunker Hill

We consider that we are all emerged in one bottom [the same boat], and must sink or swim together.... Let us all be of one heart, and stand fast in the liberty wherewith Christ has made us free; and may he of his infinite mercy grant us deliverance out of all our troubles.[33]

—Letter to citizens of Boston under British blockade, 1774

## Harriet Beecher Stowe—teacher, author, and abolitionist

A day of grace is yet held out to us. Both North and South have been guilty before God; and the Christian church has a heavy account to answer. Not by combining together, to protest injustice and cruelty, and making a common capital of sin, is this Union to be saved—but by repentance, justice and mercy.[34]

—*Uncle Tom's Cabin*

## Appendix C

# SPIRITUAL MARTYRS

THE SCRIPTURE IN Revelation 12:11—"And they loved not their lives unto the death" (KJV)— becomes a reality when we relate it to the historical leaders who gave their lives for our religious liberty. The Bible teaches that there will be a day when the persecution of believers will be at an all-time peak.

A great spiritual discipline is to pray concerning the blood that is crying out from the ground from the innocent bloodshed from martyrs from our past.

- *William Tyndale*—Strangled and burned at the stake. His last prayer was that God would open the eyes of the king of England. Twenty-five years later King James commissioned a new Bible based on Tyndale's translation.
- *John Wycliffe*—Died 1384 of natural causes. Forty years later it is noted that his ecclesiastical enemies dug his body up, burned it, and threw it into the river.
- *Lollards*—Called *Mutterers,* trained by John Wycliffe. They spoke written portions of the Bible in common English. Many were martyred.

- *Manz Grebel*—Led a group that started baptizing people, which was considered the most revolutionary act after the Protestant Reform. He was drowned in front of his mother. As he walked to the river, his mother cried out for him to stay faithful. His last words: "Into thy hand, O God, I commend my spirit." He was then thrown into the river.
- *Michael Sattler* (1527)—He had the same goal as Luther—to combat unsound teachings of his day with truth. His tongue was cut out and his flesh ripped apart. He was then burned alive.
- *John Rogers*—Killed by Bloody Mary (queen of England). He said that he would seal what he preached with his blood as his wife and children watched him being burned at the stake.
- *Group of College Graduates* (1956)—Speared to death attempting to translate the Bible to isolated people: Jim Elliot, Nate Smith, Ed McCully, Pete Fleming, and Roger Youderian
- *China and North Korea*—Persecution being endured by Christians today, with many being martyred for their belief in Christ.
- *Martin Luther*—Inspired by Erasmus, world's greatest scholar, who although not a Christian, revived the study of the ancient biblical languages of Greek and Hebrew to translate God's Word (Cyrus Anointing). On October 31, 1517, "All Saints Eve," Luther posted his ninety-five theses on the doors of Wittenberg Church as a result of running across a copy of the translated Bible and reading: "The just shall live by faith." Martin Luther died of natural causes but experienced much persecution.

## Biblical Martyrs

- *Stephen* was the first martyr.
- *James* (son of Zebedee) was beheaded ten years after Stephen's death.
- *Philip* was crucified in A.D. 54.
- *Matthew* was killed with a battle-ax.
- *James* was killed with a club.
- *Eleven of Jesus's disciples* (plus Paul) were martyred.
- *Ignatius* (Peter's successor) was ripped apart by wild beasts at the hands of the Roman authorities. While dying he said, "Now I begin to be a disciple."
- *Polycarp* (bishop of Smyrna) was asked to recant his faith in Christ. His response was, "Eighty-six years I have served Him, and He never once wronged me. How should I then blaspheme my King, who has saved me?" As his persecutors attempted to burn him alive, a fire was lit for him but miraculously could not touch him. His frustrated killers then stabbed him to death.
- *Irenaeus* (bishop of Lyons) was martyred by the Roman emperor in A.D. 202.

> And they have overcome (conquered) him by means of the blood of the Lamb and by the utterance of their testimony, for they did not love and cling to life even when faced with death [holding their lives cheap till they had to die for their witnessing].
>
> —Revelation 12:11

You have completed this phase of spiritual boot camp. You are leaving one season and entering the next. Always remember that just as doctors, lawyers, and others are licensed professionals, we are also required to have continuing education. Whether you are a minister or a brother or sister who loves Jesus, the Lord has ordained you to be an overcomer and more than a conqueror!

Stay strong in the Lord, keep the faith, and always submit yourself to your next level of training and activation.

—Apostle Kim

# NOTES

## Chapter 3
## The Importance of a Good Foundation

1. "The Army Values," Army.Mil Features, http://www.army.mil/values/ (accessed May 24, 2012).

## Chapter 11
## A Good Soldier Knows How to Stand Down

1. Tamara Lush and Greg Bluestein, Associated Press, "New Evidence Emerges as Zimmerman Appears in Court," *Columbus Dispatch*, April 12, 2012, http://www.dispatch.com/content/stories/national_world/2012/04/12/zimmerman-in-court.html (accessed May 25, 2012).

## Chapter 12
## Boot Camp Financial Principles

1. Germaine Copeland, *Prayers That Avail Much* (Tulsa, OK: Harrison House, 2000).

## Chapter 14
## The Peter Principle in the Kingdom

1. Laurence J. Peter and Raymond Hull, *The Peter Principle* (New York: HarperBusiness, 1969, 2009).

## Chapter 15
## Getting Back to Our Roots

1. Craig von Buseck, "444 Years: The Massacre of the Huguenot Christians in America," *ChurchWatch* (blog), July 2, 2008, http://blogs.cbn.com/ChurchWatch/archive/2008/07/02/444-years-the-huguenot-christians-in-america.aspx (accessed May 28, 2012). Also,

Jerry Wilkinson, "Influence of France on Florida," KeysHistory.org, http://www.keyshistory.org/FL-Fla-Fr.html (accessed May 28, 2012).

2. Charles E. Bennett, *Laudonniere and Ft. Caroline: History and Documents* (n.p.: University of Alabama Press, 2001), 14.

3. Buseck, "444 Years: The Massacre of the Huguenot Christians in America."

## Part Four
## Spiritual Battle Strategies

1. Adapted from the "US Soldier's Warrior Ethos," in Department of the Army, *Army Leadership: Competent, Confident, and Agile*, FM 6-22, October 2006, Figure 4-1, 44, http://usacac.army.mil/cac2/Repository/Materials/fm6-22.pdf (accessed May 29, 2012).

## Chapter 16
## Soldiers Against Terrorism

1. Council on Foreign Relations, "Abu Sayyaf Group (Philippines, Islamist Separarists)," May 27, 2009, http://www.cfr.org/philippines/abu-sayyaf-group-philippines-islamist-separatists/p9235 (accessed May 29, 2012).

2. CNN.com, "Bush Announces Opening of Attacks," October 7, 2001, http://articles.cnn.com/2001-10-07/us/ret.attack.bush_1_qaeda-targets-al-kandahar?_s=PM:US (accessed May 29, 2012); WhiteHouse.gov, "The U.S. Commitment to the Afghan People," http://georgewbush-whitehouse.archives.gov/infocus/backtoschool/commitment.html (accessed May 29, 2012); CNN.com, "Marines Move Into U.S. Embassy in Kabul," December 10, 2001, http://articles.cnn.com/2001-12-10/world/ret.afghan.embassy_1_kabul-embassy-diplomatic-ties-post-taliban-government?_s=PM:asiapcf (accessed May 25, 2012).

3. Encyclopedia.com, s.v. "Al-Gama'a al-Islamiyya," http://www.encyclopedia.com/article-1G2-3447100016/al-gamaa-al-islamiyya.html (accessed May 29, 2012).

4. GlobalSecurity.org, "Al-Qaida/Al-Qaeda (the Base)," http://www.globalsecurity.org/military/world/para/al-qaida.htm (accessed May 29, 2012).

5. *Tuscaloosa News*, "German Police Arrest al Tawhid Members," April 24, 2002, http://news.google.com/newspapers?nid=1817&dat=20020424&id=Ino0AAAAIBAJ&sjid=CqYEAAAAIBAJ&pg=4406,4527656 (accessed May 29, 2012).

6. USAToday.com, "Americans Flight 11 Victims at a Glance," September 25, 2001, http://www.usatoday.com/news/nation/2001/09/12/victim-capsule-flight11.htm (accessed May 29, 2012).

7. PentagonMemorial.org, "Frequently Asked Questions: How Many People Were on American Airlines Flight 77?", http://pentagonmemorial.org/plan/faq (accessed May 29, 2012).

8. GlobalSecurity.org, "Armed Islamic Group (GIA)," http://www.globalsecurity.org/military/world/para/gia.htm (accessed May 29, 2012).

9. Biography.com, "Osama bin Laden," http://www.biography.com/people/osama-bin-laden-37172 (accessed May 29, 2012).

10. FAS.org, "Convention on the Prohibition of the Development, Production and Stockpiling of Bacteriological (Biological) and Toxin Weapons and on Their Destruction," http://www.fas.org/nuke/control/bwc/text/bwc.htm (accessed May 29, 2012).

11. Christopher C. Lovett, "History Courses for Dr. Christopher C. Lovett: Glossary," Emporia State University, http://www.esuhistoryprof.com/toppage1.htm (accessed May 29, 2012).

12. Jewish Virtual Library, "Fatah," http://www.jewishvirtuallibrary.org/jsource/Terrorism/Fatah.html (accessed May 29, 2012); Jewish Virtual Library, "IDF Seizes PA Weapons Ship: The *Karine A* Affair," http://www.jewishvirtuallibrary.org/jsource/Peace/paship .html (accessed May 29, 2012).

13. *New York Times*, "Q&A: What Is the Fedayeen Saddam?", March 25, 2003, http://www.nytimes.com/cfr/international/backgroundiraq2032503.html (accessed May 29, 2012).

## Appendix B
## Boot Camp Study Notes

1. Justia.com, "*Church of the Holy Trinity v. United States*—143 U.S. 457 (1892)," http://supreme.justia.com/cases/federal/us/143/457/case.html (accessed May 30, 2012). Emphasis added.

2. United Historical and Patriotic Societies and Associations of New York, *The Need of a History of New York* (published under the auspices of the Committee of Nine, 1915), 29–30. Viewed at Google Books.

3. University of Virginia, "The Thanksgiving Proclamation, New York, 3 October 1789," The Papers of George Washington, http://gwpapers.virginia.edu/documents/thanksgiving/intro.html (accessed May 30, 2012).

4. Government Printing Office, "Washington's Farewell Address to the People of the United States," http://www.gpo.gov/fdsys/pkg/GPO-CDOC-106sdoc21/pdf/GPO-CDOC-106sdoc21.pdf (accessed May 30, 2012).

5. Edward Jewett Wheeler et al., *The Literary Digest*, vol. 12 (Lafayette Place, NY: Funk &Wagnalls Company, 1896), 20. Viewed at Google Books.

6. *The Sailor's Magazine and Naval Journal*, vol. 19–20 (n.p.: American Seamen's Friend Society, 1847), 114. Viewed at Google Books.

7. Charles Francis Adams, *The Works of John Adams, Second President of the United States*, vol. 2 (Boston: Little, Brown, and Company, 1865), 6–7. Viewed at Google Books.

8. Charles Francis Adams, *The Works of John Adams, Second President of the United States*, vol. 9 (Boston: Little, Brown, and Company, 1854), 401. Viewed at Google Books.

9. Monticello.org, "Quotations on the Jefferson Memorial," Panel Three, http://www.monticello.org/site/jefferson/quotations-jefferson-memorial (accessed May 30, 2012).

10. Bartleby.com, "James Madison: First Inaugural Address, Saturday, March 4, 1809," http://www.bartleby.com/124/pres18.html (accessed May 30, 2012).

11. The Avalon Project at Yale University, "Second Inaugural Address of James Monroe, Monday, March 5, 1821," http://avalon.law.yale.edu/19th_century/monroe2.asp (accessed May 30, 2012).

12. TeachingAmericanHistory.org, "Speech on Independence Day," http://teachingamericanhistory.org/library/index.asp?document=2337 (accessed May 30, 2012).

13. "What Scientists, Statesmen, and Great Thinkers Say of the Bible," *Primitive Methodist Magazine* 66, January 1885, 107. Viewed at Google Books.

14. The American Presidency Project, "Abraham Lincoln: Proclamation 97: Appointing a Day of National Humiliation, Fasting, and Prayer, March 30, 1863," University of California–Santa Barbara, http://www.presidency.ucsb.edu/ws/index.php?pid=69891#axzz1wNsU6ULt (accessed May 30, 2012).

15. Christian Worldview of History and Culture, "Christian Worldview of History and Culture Found in Quotes From Founding Father, and Physician, Dr. Benjamin Rush," http://www.christianworldviewofhistoryandculture.com/benjaminrushquotes (accessed May 30, 2012).

16. Christian Worldview of History and Culture, "Christian Worldview of History and Culture Found in Quotes From the Puritan Governor to the Pilgrims, William Bradford," http://www.christianworldviewofhistoryandculture.com/williambradfordquotes (accessed May 30, 2012).

17. Websters-Online-Dictionary.org, s.v. "John Hancock," Quotations, http://www.websters-online-dictionary.org/definitions/John+Hancock (accessed May 30, 2012).

18. John Rodgers, "'The Dominion of Providence Over the Works of Men,' A Sermon Preached at Princeton, on the 17th of May, 1776," in *The Works of the Rev. John Witherspoon*, vol. 2 (Philadelphia: William W. Woodward, 1800), 424. Viewed at Google Books.

19. Alexis de Tocqueville, *Democracy in America* (1835, 1840), as referenced in Thomas Lee Abshier, "Alexis de Tocqueville," DoctorSenator.com, http://www.doctorsenator.com/AlexisdeTocqueville.html (accessed May 30, 2012).

20. Attributed to Alexis de Tocqueville, "Quotes on Liberty and Virtue," http://www.liberty1.org/virtue.htm (accessed May 30, 2012).

21. Jared Sparks, *The Life of Gouverneur Morris*, vol. 3 (Boston: Gray and Bowen, 1832), 483. Viewed at Google Books.

22. John Jay, letter to John Murray, October 12, 1816, in William Jay, *The Life of John Jay*, vol. 2 (New York: J. & J. Harper, 1833), 376. Viewed at Google Books.

23. "Extracts From the Will of John Jay," in William Jay, William Jay, *The Life of John Jay*, vol. 1 (New York: J. & J. Harper, 1833), 519–520. Viewed at Google Books.

24. Benjamin Franklin, speech to the Constitutional Convention, June 28, 1787, as quoted in John Epy Lovell, *The Young* Speaker, 10th edition (New Haven, CT: Durrie & Peck, 1849), 165. Viewed at Google Books.

25. As quoted in William Joseph Federer, *America's God and Country: Encyclopedia of Quotations* (n.p.: Amerisearch, Inc., 1994), 560.

26. Alexander Hamilton, John Jay, and James Madison, *The Federalist and Other Contemporary Papers on the Constitution of the United States* (New York: Scott, Foresman and Company, 1894), 646. Viewed at Google Books.

27. As quoted in Federer, *America's God and Country: Encyclopedia of Quotations*, 456–457.

28. Ibid., 143.

29. Samuel Adams, "The Rights of the Colonists as Christians," in William Vincent Wells, *The Life and Public Services of Samuel Adams*, vol. 1 (Boston: Little, Brown and Company, 1865), 504. Viewed at Google Books.

30. Joseph Story, *The Miscellaneous Writings: Literary, Critical, Judicial, and Political* (Boston: James Munroe and Company, 1835), 60. Viewed at Google Books.

31. Edwin Percy Whipple, *The Great Speeches and Orations of Daniel Webster* (Boston: Little, Brown and Company, 1886), 51. Viewed at Google Books.

32. William Wirt, *Sketches of the Life and Character of Patrick Henry* (Philadelphia: James Webster, 1817), 58. Viewed at Google Books.

33. As quoted in Abram English Brown, *Beside Old Hearth-Stones* (Boston: Lee and Shepard Publishers, 1897), 22–23. Viewed at Google Books.

34. Harriet Beecher Stowe, *Uncle Tom's Cabin* (n.p.: Forgotten Books, 1962), 525. Viewed at Google Books.

★★★★★

# SPIRITUAL WARFARE IS REAL!

**There is a spiritual battle going on, and Satan does not play fairly. Be encouraged and challenged by the no-holds-barred style of Kimberly Daniels in all of her books.**

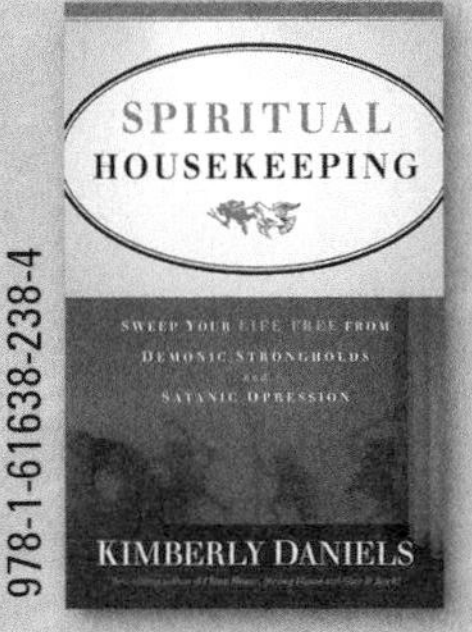


978-1-61638-238-4

978-0-88419-964-9

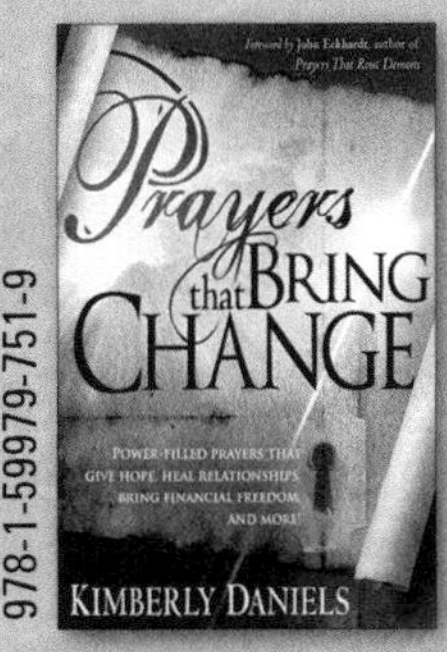


978-1-59979-751-9

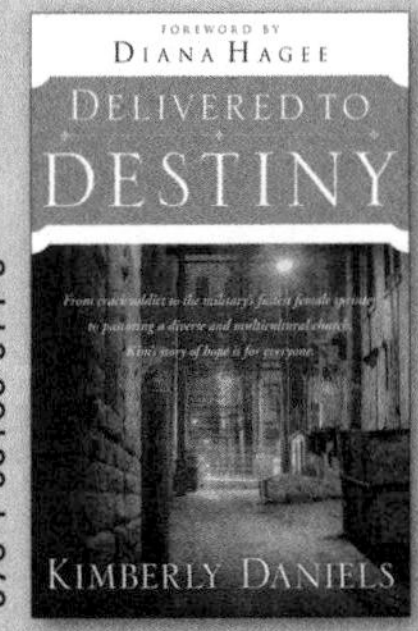


978-1-59185-614-6

978-1-59979-057-2

978-1-59979-279-8

978-0-88419-935-9

★★★★★

AVAILABLE WHEREVER CHRISTIAN BOOKS ARE SOLD

WWW.CHARISMAHOUSE.COM
WWW.FACEBOOK.COM/CHARISMAHOUSE